The New Phrase Book

MW01515704

Old Sayings, Expressions & Odd Names of New Brunswick

Dan Soucoup

Pottersfield Press, Lawrencetown Beach, Nova Scotia, Canada

Library and Archives Canada Cataloguing in Publication

Soucoup, Dan, 1949-

The New Brunswick phrase book : old sayings, expressions and odd names of New Brunswick / Dan Soucoup.

ISBN 1-895900-84-0

1. Canadianisms (English) – New Brunswick. 2. Aphorisms and apothegms – New Brunswick. 3. Names, Geographical – New Brunswick. I. Title.

FC2454.S69 2006   971.5'1   C2006-903761-2

Front cover photo: George Fischer Photography
Cover design: Gail Leblanc

Pottersfield Press acknowledges the ongoing support of The Canada Council for the Arts, as well as the Nova Scotia Department of Tourism, Culture and Heritage, Cultural Affairs Division. We also acknowledge the financial support of the Government of Canada through the Book Publishing Industry Development Program for our publishing activities.

Pottersfield Press
83 Leslie Road
East Lawrencetown
Nova Scotia, Canada, B2Z 1P8
Website: www.pottersfieldpress.com
To order, phone 1-800-NIMBUS9 (1-800-646-2879)
Printed in Canada

Acknowledgements

The bulk of this collection has been assembled over time from various places, including oral and written sources too numerous to document. Yet some of the material was gleaned from a number of well-known written sources by writers who have researched various aspects of the use of language in New Brunswick. These writers include W.F. Ganong, Alan Rayburn, William B. Hamilton, Stuart Trueman, Herb Curtis, David Mazerolle, Lori Baker, B.J. Grant, George Frederick Clarke, Murray Stewart, Louise Manny, and James Reginald Wilson. I would like to especially thank David Goss for contributing a number of entries to this project. His story about moving the horse on Mecklenburg Street is one of my favourites.

Introduction

In the velvet, uplifters, bang bellies, wangan, and the walking boss. Restigouche Sam or Restigouche Toothpick? And what about Tanty-Wanty, waterhaul, or bare pole versus a setting-pole? What's the difference between the Big Hawk and the big house, a boondoggle, calibogus, or cockaninny? We may know the distinction between a box lunch and a bed lunch, but what about bushed and a boom, a camp as distinct from a cottage? Both contact men and preventatives were government appointees in New Brunswick during the Great Depression but what's a platform man? If we think we know New Brunswick, then is it cuffer down or come-uppance? Couple a few or couple a dozen? A gawker and a geezer, gorby and Gorney, hello fer going at Mistake Cove or was it Disappointment Lake?

These strange names and sayings were once widely used in New Brunswick. How people speak can tell us a lot about a community, and the expressions they use are even more revealing. So too are the names and nicknames that bring to mind one-of-a-kind descriptions of places and events.

What we speak in New Brunswick is a fascinating assortment of expressions, phrases, old sayings, and odd lingo, and this language is a mixture of contemporary culture and historical influences. Some of what is collected here relates to everyday life and can be heard in various parts of North America. But much of what appears in these pages is fairly exclusive to the province and has been derived from the uniqueness of New Brunswickers and where they live.

In assembling this compilation of more than one thousand New Brunswickisms, I have tried to find sayings, expressions, and odd names that are a bit different and exclusive to the province. But I also extended the search to phrases and names that would have been used in New Brunswick or are still in use despite the fact that the terms may have originated elsewhere. It is quite difficult to know if "free pour" originated in the province (it didn't) or "cockaninny" (it probably did) but what is interesting, I think, is that both expressions are used in New Brunswick along with a host of other extremely strange and intriguing terms such as stumping, yangin, yarding, setting the dogs, blueberry dog-bellies, billycan, sacking, and dunnage.

Place names in New Brunswick are also quite interesting. George Frederick Clarke remarked that the province's rivers all seemed to have "strange, strong, fascinating names" such as Restigouche, Upsalquitch, Tobique, Magaguadavic, Miramichi, and perhaps the oddest of them all, Skoodowabskook. And bold and somewhat odd place names are also apparent such as Apohaqui, Beaubears, Cape Enrage, Kennebecasis, and Napadogan.

Political slogans revealed interesting details about the past and I have included a number of old election slogans, the majority of which will be still remembered today. While the term "Smashers" would not be familiar currently, anyone involved in politics in the 1950s would remember the campaign rallying cries "Let's Clean House" or "Carry

On Hugh John." Similarly, who could forget the slogan "Equal Opportunity" during the 1960s, and most Saint Johners in the early 1980s would remember Elsie Wayne's slogan: "Elephant Never Forgets – How About You?" In the late 1980s, "We the People" became the familiar slogan of the Confederation of Regions party, and the "Madawaska Weaver" became a derogatory phrase associated with the Conservative leader during the 1995 Liberal re-election victory of Frank McKenna.

It should be no surprise that the largest collection of phrases comes out of the old lumber business, still New Brunswick's biggest industry. Some great examples are swampers, shims and shooks, Kennebecker, thirty for a thousand, a twitching horse, scantling line, breaking the jam, and Main John. But phrases from the offshore fishing industry are also prominent, including counters and bobs, herring stringer, kipperin', bushed, and bugging. In addition, salmon fishing has its own unusual vocabulary with terms such as greased line, gillie, raising a boil, Dryfly Ramsey, and one minute to the pound.

Expressions such as time to feed the hay, potato belt, and frost on the pumpkin come from the farming sector and one of the most interesting times for inventive language seems to have been the Prohibition Era (1920-1933), when the varied and ingenious ways of drinking illegal alcohol gave rise to marvellous terms such as another dead soldier, cab-driver gin, fly beer, Jakey, panther piss, and canned heat.

Railways were once everywhere in New Brunswick and wonderful old phrases such as bo money, sleepers, wigwag, came on the freight, hump yard, stroker, shorts, shimshack, shoofly, seenar, and trimmer could be heard in most communities where the old steam locomotives (locos) came and went. Creative names for food and favourite recipes are also intriguing. Some of the phrases reveal plenty of imagination such as slip and go easy pancakes, or potatoes in their jackets, chicken bones, sit-down supper, pot-en-pot, and sex-in-a-pan. And what about Richibucto goose or maybe Shippagan turkey served with Yankee toast and bean-hole baked beans?

Expressions about nature and wildlife are also common such as rutting time, droppings, foxes in the henhouse, moose fly, lampers, devil's darning needle, and gorby. Business expressions are plentiful: the man behind the plow, drummers, city with natural gas, and I like to see the wheels turning. Phrases describing crime and punishment include get wigged, hoosegow, hue and cry, jacking, line-house, Joe Walnut, and the beer bandit caper. Political terminology includes muckraking, on with the dance, 1-800-McKenna, Good Roads Veniot, and the Three Musketeers.

Weather terms are popular: flood talk, storm-stayed, old-fashioned nor'easter, lightning seeks water, and mackerel sky is not long dry. Religious expressions include fire and brimstone, down-I-lay-me's, rage for dipping, backsliding, and New Canaan. Cursing and swearing also make contributions to New Brunswickers' colourful use of language such as jesiless, sonofa'hore, friggit, and for cripe's sake. And let's not forget sexual expressions such as grassin', piece of tail, clap, getting your skin, hard on, and making out.

Since New Brunswick is a bilingual province, I have included some French phrases such as Tétines de souris, aboiteau, and joie de vivre, and French-English slang expressions such as che mess and Hi, ça va. As well, I have noted many Aboriginal terms such as Chip-la-kwa-gun and Skoodowabskook. Finally, I have added quite a number of odd expressions that defy categorization but are a treasure trove of insights about New Brunswick and its people. Examples are biggest east of Montreal, quill her, girl who rouges, gawgaw, and it was no do.

In reading through this lexicon, I expect many of these phrases and expressions could become adopted by the reader and reused again, perhaps even changed slightly to describe something new, a cultural pastime or business enterprise. So much the better and please, go right at it.

A

Aboiteau – Acadian dykes that were first erected in the seventeenth century to drain the tidal marshes around the Bay of Fundy.

Ah c'mon – How about reconsidering?

Albertite – A mineral identified as solidified bitumen and unique to Albert County. The shale is similar to coal and was first discovered in the Turtle Creek area by Abraham Gesner, a physician, geologist, and inventor. Dr. Gesner (1797-1864) was the first provincial geologist and the inventor of kerosene.

Alden – Alden Nowlan, New Brunswick's renowned poet. Nowlan (1933-1983) is an iconic figure in Canadian literature. The noted critic Robert Bly refers to Nowlan as the greatest Canadian poet of the twentieth century.

Alders – Troublesome little trees that form into thickets along streams and make fishing the best trout holes difficult. How to get rid of alders is a hot topic of conversation in rural New Brunswick according to the magazine *Rural Delivery*.

All cold potatoes – Water under the bridge, irrelevant now.

All cool eh? – New Brunswick Liquor Company called Alcool NB Liquor.

All Day All Night Camp Grounds – Black River Bridge campsite.

All hands out – Longshoremen's expression for all workers are on the job.

All hell broke loose – A small issue that became a big problem.

All nerved – Uptight or on edge.

All played out – Tired.

All tuckered out – Tired, played out.

Almshouse – Kings County brook that flows into the Kennebecasis River.

A'lowfer deer – Hello for deer, as in a whole lot of deer sighted.

Alpine – The most popular beer in New Brunswick, brewed in Saint John by Moosehead. Moosehead Beer is a close second.

Andy's Dummy Farm – Unique and humorous exhibition of dummy characters at Andy MacDonald's place near Port Elgin.

Angland – England.

Another dead soldier – Empty bottle of alcohol.

Ant – Aunt.

An' they built 'em in th' cricks – In the nineteenth century's Golden Age of Sail, shipbuilders built big square-rigged vessels in the little tidal creeks along the Bay of Fundy.

Antzy – Can't relax, being on edge.

Apohaqui – This Kings County community was originally known as Mouth of Millstream by early Loyalist settlers but reverted to its Maliseet name in the mid-1850s. The probable translation is "mouth of stream."

Are – Our, as in "This is are new house."

Are you going to a funeral? – Why are you in a hurry?

Aroostook – River that flows into the St. John River in Victoria County. Origin of the name is uncertain.

Arse end – Back side.

Arvin's – The original Irving general store in Bouctouche. "To see Christmas comin', we jus' had to watch 'em Arvin's window," says *La Sagouine* by Antonine Maillet. (See also K.C. and La Sagouine)

Assburns – Aspirins.

ATV – Most watched TV station but also most popular all-terrain motor vehicle for off-road activities.

Aulac – Border-crossing point with Nova Scotia. The name was derived from the French Le Lac, where prior to 1755, an Acadian village by that name was located at the head of Rivière-du-Lac.

Awful good – Extremely good.

B

Babes in the woods – Innocents, capable of being duped. The phrase originated in Britain. But the expression became commonplace in the Maritimes after a tragic situation occurred near Halifax, Nova Scotia, where two children were lost in the woods and perished. A song about the incident – "The Lost Babes of Halifax" – was sung at one of the first Miramichi Folk Festivals.

Backsliding – Baptist expression for sinning, forgetting about one's faith, or returning to evil ways.

Bad tear – On a big booze spree.

BAG – The Beaverbrook Art Gallery in Fredericton.

Bag on – Loaded. Also, in the bag.

Baie des Chaleurs – French for the Bay of Heat, it was named by explorer Jacques Cartier, who arrived during a warm period in July of 1534.

Baie Verte – A village and bay near the Nova Scotia border. The name derives from the saltwater grasses that grow each summer, giving the appearance of a green meadow.

Ball of wax – The whole thing.

Balsam Fir – New Brunswick's official tree.

Barachois – A Westmorland County village near Shediac. Probably of Basque origin and a common place name throughout Atlantic Canada (eight times in New Brunswick alone), it means a coastal, saltwater pond or inlet protected from the sea by a sandbar.

Bare pole – Naked male.

Bark – Your bark is your voice.

Barrel-piled – Sawed logs that were piled up at a landing without skids (poles laid counter to the logs in order to keep the timber dry) inserted between rows. A skidded landing meant that each row of logs in a pile was separated by skids.

Bartibog – A river that flows into the Miramichi on the north side below Newcastle. The name appears to have been derived from a Mi'kmaq chief named Bartholomew LaBogue.

Batterst – Bathurst. A city in the northeastern part of the province, named in 1826 in honour of the British Colonial Secretary, Henry, Third Earl of Bathurst.

Bay du Vin – Bay of Winds. A community and bay in Northumberland County on the south shore of Miramichi Bay.

Bay of Fundy – Called Baye Françoise by Samuel de Champlain in 1604 and Bakudabakek by the Passamaquoddy people. The present name may have come from Portuguese fishermen who named it "fondo," meaning deep.

Bean-hole baked beans – Traditional Miramichi baked beans with salt pork in a crock. The beans are placed in a hole in the ground on top of red hot embers, covered over with earth and left overnight. It makes a delicious meal the next morning.

Beats carrying sardines – Prohibition-era slogan from the 1920s that originated with fishermen along the Bay of Fundy who traded in their fishing activities for the more lucrative rum-running.

Beaubears – An island in the Miramichi River above Newcastle where about 3,500 Acadian refugees gathered after the Expulsion of 1755 under the protection of French military officer Charles Deschamps de Boishébert.

The Beav – Lord Beaverbrook Hotel in Fredericton. Now the Crowne Plaza Fredericton Lord Beaverbrook.

The Beaver – Lord Beaverbrook, Sir William Maxwell (Max) Aitken (1879-1964) from Newcastle. Also called Britain's Beaver since he made a name for himself during the Battle of Britain. The Ontario-born, New Brunswick-raised preacher's son became a millionaire businessman.

Bed lunch – Snack before going to bed.

Beer Bandit Caper – Infamous case of a missing truck with 50,000 cans of Moosehead beer that was headed for Mexico and mysteriously disappeared in August 2004. The story was immortalized in *The Beer Bandit Caper: The Mounties, Their Man & Mexico's Missing Moosehead* by Harvey Sawler.

Bejesus – The guts, as in to beat the bejesus out of him.

Beloved Isle – American President Franklin Delano Roosevelt's nickname for his favourite island, Campobello, where he maintained a summer home.

The Bend – Moncton's early name, as in the Bend of the Petitcodiac. Also called Le Coude, meaning the elbow.

Benedict Arnold – Turncoat, traitor, and all-round bad guy of the American Revolution, burned in effigy by the people of Saint John who didn't like his arrogant manner or his business practices. He lived in Saint John from 1787 to 1791.

Bennett buggies – Cars hauled by horses during the Depression. R.B. Bennett from Hopewell Hill was Canada's eleventh prime minster and the only one from New Brunswick. As the leader of Canada during the Great Depression, he became associated with bad news, including the lack of money to buy gasoline.

Bent out of shape – Angry or sometimes drunk and angry.

Best dulse in the world – At Dark Harbour on the western side of Grand Manan Island, high cliffs on three sides protect the harbour and this lack of sunlight produces some of the richest marine algae in the Bay of Fundy, including the highly prized seaweed called dulse.

Big axe – The world's largest axe, located at Nackawic, comprised of seven tons of steel and representing the province's largest industry – forestry.

Big Bald – One of New Brunswick's highest mountains in Northumberland County. At 2,205 feet (672 metres) it's the highest point in the Miramichi River range.

Big blow – Big talker, little substance or perhaps a liar, as in, "He's a big blow."

Big Cove Elsipogtog First Nation – Mi'kmaq First Nation

and largest Aboriginal reserve in New Brunswick at Big Cove near Bouctouche.

Big feeling – Someone who's pretentious.

Biggest east of Montreal – Very popular unit of measure.

Big Hawk – Shikatehawk Stream that flows into the St. John River at Bristol. Derived from the Maliseet Shigateehawg that can be translated as "where he killed him," referring to an old Mohawk-Maliseet battle that was won by the Maliseet. A smaller branch called the Little Hawk also joins the St. John River at this junction.

Big house – Dorchester Penitentiary or "The Pen." Now the prison at Renous is the big house.

Big jag – Large piece or load, as in a jag of wood.

Billycan – All-purpose metal water can that serves as a canteen and a kettle.

Black-capped chickadee – New Brunswick's provincial bird.

Black hole of Calcutta – Really bad place where you could be sent as a child if you didn't behave. The term refers to a 1756 incident in India when a large number of people were confined overnight in a small cell at Fort William in Calcutta and all but twenty-three died.

Black Horse Tavern – Famous old drinking establishment in Newcastle and the inspiration for a 1973 book of short stories of the same name by New Brunswick writer Ray Fraser.

Black salmon – Fish that have already laid eggs and are going downriver. Not great eating, as opposed to bright salmon that are going upriver to spawn. Other names for black salmon include slinks, racers, kelts, and spent fish.

Black Wednesday – Tragic day in 1877 when more than 1,600 homes burned in the Great Saint John Fire. On June 20 the downtown business and residential district – 243 acres or ninety-eight hectares – was destroyed, eighteen people died and 15,000 were left homeless. Damage was estimated at $25 million. Reconstruction began almost immediately and within four years more than a thousand buildings had been constructed.

Blind baggage – Old hobo term for riding secretly on a train in the baggage department. Hobos hoped to remain undetected in the baggage area since there was no gangway access to the rest of the train.

Blind pig – Unlicensed liquor bar and illegal after-hours club.

Bloaters – Hard-cured (six to ten weeks of salting and drying) herring from the Bay of Fundy that were packed in eighteen-pound boxes and shipped to the West Indies.

Blow down – Section of a wooden trail closed over due to fallen trees.

Blow-me-down – Abrupt headland.

Blow the roost – To get away quickly.

Blueberry dog-belly – A dessert that consists of rolled-up biscuit dough and blueberries in a cheesecloth and then boiled on the top of a stove. Bang bellies are blueberry dumplings.

Blueberry Special – Grand Southern Railway train that ran daily between Saint John and St. Stephen and cut through a large blueberry bog near Pennfield Ridge, where pickers could jump on and off the train almost at will.

Blue streak – Very fast, as in charging out in a blue streak.

Board foot – Standard piece of lumber measuring twelve inches long, twelve inches wide, and one inch thick. To find the number of board feet in a piece of lumber, multiple the thickness by the width and the length, and then divide by twelve.

Bogan – Backwater channel, or still water behind or adjoining a river. The word comes from Aboriginal sources and is popular in northern New Brunswick with thirty names that include bogans, such as Mersereau Bogan and Fanton Bogan.

Bo money – Money collected on the sly from hobos by freight train crews in the 1930s, allowing them to secretly ride on the trains. (See also Boxcar tourists)

Boom – A chain of floating logs gathered together end-to-end. The boom contains a whole mess of logs that are floated together as a raft downriver on a drive.

Boondoggle – A scam or public scandal and, of course, highly controversial.

Bootleg – Any form of illegal selling of liquor but the term originated in the lumber industry prior to 1900 when larrigans (waterproof leather moccasins) were popular. Bottles of liquor could be stashed in the tops of the larrigans and smuggled with ease, thus accounting for the "bootleg" concept.

The Bore – Tidal wave that comes up the Petitcodiac River twice daily at Moncton and is considered aptly named by most Monctonians.

Boss Gibson – Alexander "Boss" Gibson (1819-1913), once the largest industrialist in New Brunswick. He controlled the mill town of Marysville and ran it like a feudal lord.

Boston States – New England.

Bouctouche – A river, town, dune, and bay. Translated from the Mi'kmaq as "big bay."

Boulevard on the Floor of the Ocean – A broad sandy bar about one mile long between the mainland and Minister's Island outside St. Andrews. At high tide the bar is covered with up to twenty feet of water, but at low tide the bar serves as a highway to the old Van Horne estate on the island. Sir William Cornelius Van Horne (1843-1915) supervised construction of Canada's transcontinental railway and had his summer home – Covenhoven – on the island.

Boxcar tourists – Hobos who rode the railcars en masse in search of work during the 1930s.

Box lunch – Take away or portable lunch.

Boys-town – Boiestown on the Southwest Miramichi River, the geographic centre of the province. It's named after Thomas Boies, who established a lumber mill in the area.

Brakie – Railway brakeman.

Brandies – Sunken rocks in a river or lake that can catch a boat and damage the hull.

Bread and molasses – All New Brunswickers ate for most of the first half of the twentieth century according to Port Elgin storyteller Andy MacDonald.

Breaking the jam – Breaking up a logjam was dangerous and in New Brunswick, going out Sunday mornings to break the jam (instead of attending church) was considered bad luck. In the famous folksong "The Jam on Gerry's Rock," a shanty boy went to his watery grave trying to clear a jam pile on a Sunday morning.

Bricklin – A bankrupt sports car manufacturing operation from the 1970s under the Richard Hatfield government that cost the provincial taxpayers $23 million. Jokes, songs, and a book made the boondoggle famous and the term became synonymous with unreal expectations or a gap in reality. As H.A. Fredericks and Allan Chambers in their book *Bricklin* put it, "The divergence between what Bricklin said about his car (the promotion) and what was actually happening (the business) became complete in the summer of 1975."

Brick short of a load – Not all there but don't give up, there's promise. Not the smartest person in the crowd.

Bridal suite – The cell in the old York County Jail in Fredericton that contained two cots.

Bristol Hawk – New breed of seed potato recently developed in the Bristol area of the upper St. John River valley.

Brow – Logs piled up beside the river waiting for the ice to melt and the spring drive to begin.

Brown-noser – Not your own person. A person who is up the behind of someone they are taking direction from. Also, a suckhole.

Brown Sugar Scow – Acadian dessert (Scow au Sucre Brun) from Gloucester County around Tracadie that comes out of the oven with a flat bottom that resembles the flat-bottomed scow boat.

Bugging – Fishing around Grand Manan where a line of hooks a foot and a half apart are dropped over in deep water with weights while the boat is drifting. As the boat drifts over the edge of a shoal, the lures (bugs) move in among pollock and with the right timing, a lot of fish can be caught. Also, bugging is a term for fly-fishing salmon with flies resembling bugs.

Bunkhouse – Roughly built log house for lumberjacks and the name of a popular country music group from the 1950s, the Bunkhouse Boys.

Burning ship – From the Phantom Ship Legend on the Baie des Chaleurs that many people claim they have seen.

Burnt Church – The name comes from a true incident. After the fall of the French fortress at Louisbourg in 1758, an English military force captured and burned a village at this site on Miramichi Bay that included a stone church.

Bushed – Bushing the hole, as in forming a windbreak around an ice-fishing hole by piling fir or spruce trees around the site. Brush weirs were another operation that involved piling evergreens along a tidal flat to direct fish into an enclosure.

Bushwhack – To travel through the woods without following a trail. Bushwhacking means following a compass bearing or landmarks on a dead reckoning without staying on a fixed line or path.

Butternut Ridge – Original name for Havelock and named after the butternut tree that is native to the area.

By the skin of your teeth – Getting by on a very small margin.

C

Cab-driver gin – An expression indicating bad liquor that originated in Prohibition during the 1920s when many taxi operators bootlegged moonshine and rot-gut alcohol. Also known as bathwater gin.

Calibogus – An odd tasting mixture of West Indies rum and spruce beer.

Call me Captain from now on! – Molly Kool's celebrated 1939 telegram to her sister in Alma after passing her master's certificate, making her North America's first female sea captain.

Calling a spade a spade – Straight shooter, telling it like it is.

Came on the freight – Small passenger sections on freight trains were common before World War I. In winter, a coal stove was often provided for warmth.

Camp – A revered possession and must be near fresh water to be a camp, as opposed to a cottage. It can be a huge and luxurious river lodge and still be a camp.

Camp Utopia – Old World War II Department of National Defence army base near Lake Utopia in Charlotte County that was surrounded by a huge blueberry bog. The recruits were officially forbidden to eat the wild berries but ate them anyway.

Canned heat – Fuel in cans sold in the early 1900s under the name Sterno, which was used to heat portable heaters and camp stoves. But canned heat to an alcoholic was very cheap, plentiful and, when cut fifty percent with water, was still one of the most potent and popular alcoholic substitutes ever seen in Depression-era New Brunswick.

Can of worms – Real mess.

Canter off – Logs in a boom could be cantered off by gathering them up one by one with a peavey or cant-dog (a stick with a prying hook at one end) and sent downriver.

Can't hack it – Can't put up with it as opposed to "hackin' 'er," which means that you can keep it going despite the pressure.

Can't see for looking – Trying to see it or understand something but having a hard time.

Can't take it to the bank – May be nice and the right thing to do but isn't practical.

Cape Bald – Old English name for Cap-Pelé. The coastal community is situated in Westmorland County along the Northumberland Strait. Cap-Pelé is the largest exporter of smoked herring in North America.

Cape Brûlé – Westmorland County point on the Northumberland Strait. Name is French for "burnt."

Cape Enrage – Cape of Rage, one of the earliest French names along the Bay of Fundy, whose name was due to the stormy weather.

Cape Maringouin – Southern tip of Westmorland County that juts out into Chignecto Bay. Named after a huge infestation of mosquitoes that Europeans first witnessed when sailing near the cape.

Captain – Nickname for Lord Beaverbrook's eccentric British friend Michael Wardell, a fiery Tory, who became the owner and publisher of the Fredericton *Daily Gleaner*.

Carousing – Up to no good, partying and drinking.

Carry on Hugh John – Conservative campaign slogan for the 1956 provincial election that saw Premier Hugh John Flemming returned to office.

Cass – La Caisse Populaire. These pioneer credit unions, first established in 1901 in Levis, Quebec, have flourished throughout Acadian New Brunswick.

Celestial city – Fredericton, home of poet Sir Charles G.D. Roberts, who called it "my city, Fredericton, a jewel in a dream." The provincial capital earned the nickname "celestial" in 1845 when a new bishopric based in Fredericton was carved out of the old diocese of Nova Scotia.

Chamcook – Near St. Andrews and from the Passamaquoddy K'tchumcook. However, no one is certain of the Aboriginal meaning.

Champlain Place – Mall in Dieppe named after the famous explorer Samuel de Champlain.

Charles "God Damn" Roberts – Renowned but cranky writer who insisted on people remembering his two middle initials G.D. (George Douglas) as God Damn. Roberts (1860-1943) is viewed as the "Father of Canadian poetry."

Cheapskate – Tightwad, stingy.

Che mess – French-English slang for "What a mess!"

Chemin Gorge Road – Bilingual road sign outside Moncton.

Chicken bones – Ganong Company's popular Christmas candy. Canada's oldest candy company introduced the cinnamon-flavoured, pink hard candy jacket over a chocolate centre in 1885.

Chickens coming home to roost – What's due. Final reckoning.

Chinwag – A good chinwag is an engaging discussion.

Chip-la-kwa-gun – A three-sided, wooden frame Aboriginal invention that held a kettle or pot suspended over an open cooking fire. A chip-la-kwa-gun is composed of two wooden sticks on each side of the fire pounded into the ground with y-shaped tops. A sturdy piece of wood is then suspended across the fire to hold the pot above the fire.

Chiputneticook Lakes – Lakes that flow into the St. Croix River along the New Brunswick-Maine border. The name is derived from the Passamaquoddy, an Aboriginal people who occupied the Passamaquoddy Bay area and were associated with the Maliseet nation. The five lakes are East Grand, Spednic, North, Palfrey, and Mud Lakes.

Chock full – Full to the brim.

Chocolate river – Petitcodiac River, whose name is derived from the Mi'kmaq Pet-koot-koy-ek that means "river that bends back." During the French and English periods in colonial history the river had numerous names, including Petcoucoyek and Petticoat Jack.

Chopper – A skilled axe-man who could fall a tree within inches of a designated spot. Some of the bigger timber camps also hired "fallers" whose special skill was helping choppers fall trees straight down.

Chopping – A cutting or clearing in the woods where trees or branches are down.

Christmas Daddies – Annual TV charity event that raises money for underprivileged children.

Christmas Mountains – Tallest peaks at Mount Carleton Provincial Park near North Pole Stream.

City of stately elms – Fredericton, for its beautiful tree-lined streets.

City with natural gas – Old 1920s slogan promoting Moncton as the only Maritime city with a local supply of natural gas. However, the gas didn't last.

Clap – Venereal disease, as in "Got the clap." Also called a dose.

Clean forgot about it – Didn't remember.

Clinker – Jail, also called gaol in the nineteenth century.

Close the lights – Turn off the lights.

C'mere right now – Come here now.

Cocagne – A town, harbour, river, cape, and island in New Brunswick. An old word meaning "utopia" in French probably because of Acadian Governor Nicolas Denys' seventeenth-century description of the place. "Having passed a little island, one is under shelter, and finds water enough . . . I have named this place River of Cocagne because I found so much with which to make good cheer during the eight days which bad weather obliged me to remain here."

Cockaninny – Home brew. Name can be traced to the Miramichi.

Codfish and taters – Essential part of an old-fashioned New Brunswick breakfast that also included fried ham, hot rolls, and pancakes, all prepared while the tea kettle is starting to boil on a cold winter morning.

Codiac – Short form for Petitcodiac that is named for regional transit and policing services around Moncton.

Coffeemill – The whirlpool at Grand Falls that used to trap logs during the old St. John River log drives. The whirlpool could grind logs into small pointed sticks.

Cold enough? – Really cold.

Cold July means hunger by and by – Old proverb in weather prediction.

Coleman frog – A forty-two-pound stuffed frog-like animal in the York-Sunbury Museum in Fredericton.

The Coliseum – Moncton's exhibition centre on Killam Drive.

Collect No Revenue – CNR, Canadian National Railway. A Depression-era slogan that originated in Moncton, depicting the financial prospects of Canada's national railway. The CNR was run as a make-work operation throughout much of the 1930s.

Come all ye's – The start of many local folksongs, especially those popular along the Miramichi.

Come from away – Person not born or brought up here.

Come rutting time – Fall mating season when big buck deer and moose come into heat and thrash around the woods.

Come-uppance – Just rewards, as in tit for tat, or the final reconciliation.

Come wider – To make a wider path or road.

Constipation cure – Drink senna tea.

Contact men – Key operators in the Depression-era political patronage system and the politics of paving. These placemen acted as employment and political agents for all workers on public projects, especially road construction.

Cookee – Cook's helper or assistant.

Cooper – Barrel and cask maker.

COR – Anti-bilingual Confederation of Regions provincial political party that broke away from the Conservative Party in the late 1980s and remained a political force for a few years before collapsing in the mid-1990s.

Cord trail – Trail made out of cord logs laid sideways to allow crossing a swampy area. Also known as a corduroy road.

Cordwood – Wood so called because the uniform length logs formed the measure (four feet by four feet by eight feet) of a cord.

Corn fritters with maple syrup – Favourite meal of regular patrons at old York's Restaurant in Andover, Victoria County.

Corporation drive – For many years each spring, the biggest single log drive in New Brunswick took place along the Restigouche River where the Fraser companies would organize a drive that would entail floating more than 300,000 cords of pulpwood down the river. In its heyday, the corporation drive was bossed by "Big Jim" Fitzgerald, who many said could have held his own against "Main John" Glasier. (See also Main John)

Cottage – Building by the shore, but must be near salt water or else it is a camp.

Cottage Craft – Grace Helen Mowat's business at St. Andrews, which she started in 1915. It still operates today. She helped establish a craft renaissance in Canada during the 1920s.

Count one out of ten – Bad count of logs by a scaler (timber counter) who was unwilling to give full credit to log producers and thus would only give credit for one log out of ten.

Counters and bobs – Old Bay of Fundy terms for large and small lobsters. Bobs were undersize and thrown back to sea. Today, large lobsters are known as markets and the smallest legal-size lobsters are canners.

Counting your chickens before they are hatched – Making a decision before all the facts are in.

Couple a dozen – Lots.

Couple a few – Not many.

Crazy as the birds – Not in your right mind.

Crick – Creek or small stream.

Crimson Beauty – New Brunswick's very own apple, originally called Early Scarlet and first introduced in Carleton County by pioneer horticulturalist Francis Sharp of Woodstock. Sharp developed this winter hardy apple in the mid-1880s. It's one of the first apples to ripen in late July or early August.

Crook's Point – York County community whose name has been traced back to the nickname of an early settler, Jean Cyr.

Crowbar hotel – Jailhouse.

Cruising – Searching the woods for mature timber to cut.

Crystal Palace – Moncton's indoor playground and Atlantic Canada's best known indoor amusement park with a roller coaster, an eighteen-hole miniature golf course, ferris wheel, and other diversions.

Cuck it up – Puke.

Cuffer down – An old square dance holler around the Nashwaak River Valley according to Murray Stewart in his book *Cuffer Down, Expressions From the Nashwaak & Over North*.

Cup'a – Cup of tea.

Cure for the hot flashes – Urine from a pregnant mare.

Cuss – To swear. Also, a naughty person, as in "He is a selfish cuss."

Cut her thin – Derogatory term for a scaler who would overcalculate the number of trees required to make a thousand feet of lumber.

Cut of your jib – Borrowed sailor's expression for your appearance, as in "I don't like the cut of your jib."

Cut off your nose to spite your face – Damned if you do and screwed if you don't.

D

Dalton – Dalton Camp was a talented journalist and Conservative Party backroom political strategist. Camp (1920-2002) initially came to public attention for his role in instigating the first political leadership review in Canada, when Prime Minister John Diefenbaker was ousted from power in the 1960s.

Danny Burger – Big burger served at Danny's Inn near Bathurst on Route 134.

Dark Lantern Brigade – Conservative nickname during the 1920s for three men who reorganized the provincial Liberal party and led it back to power: Peter Veniot, E.S. (Ned) Carter, and Frank Carvell.

Deacon's bench – Log cut in half with legs attached to serve as furniture in a lumber camp.

Deader than a doornail – Positively dead.

Deadhead – Railway term for an employee or relative travelling free on a pass.

Deadwater – Any still section of water can be called deadwater but in New Brunswick, the phrase is also used to describe smooth but slow-flowing sections of a river. (See also Bogan)

Deadwood – Rotted tree stump or piece of lumber but also a slack worker.

Deaf as a doornail – Very hard of hearing.

Deal – Cut spruce, fir, or pine lumber that was exported to Britain. Standard sizes for deals were three inches thick, nine inches wide, and twelve feet long.

Death warmed over – Pretty far gone.

Deck'm high – Logs piled high up on the skid.

Deluxe French Fries – Fried food chain that started with a chip wagon in downtown Moncton.

Demon rum – All alcohol during the Prohibition Era when temperance societies equated alcoholic beverages with the Devil.

Devil's Back – Near Colepaugh Brook in York County. A devil's back is a ridge or ledge halfway up a steep slope. Devil's Back Brook flows into the St. John River in Kings County near Victoria Beach. Twelve place names in New Brunswick include devil in their names.

Devil's darning needle – Dragon fly that could sew up a child's mouth if they were noisy, naughty, or told lies.

Devil's half acre – Old nineteenth-century nickname for Dorchester. As the political capital of Westmorland, the village of Dorchester, "the corner" or "square" as it was called, contained a half-acre of parish buildings, a court-house, probate and record office, post office, telegraph office, private legal offices, and grog (liquor) shops. Thus, the nickname: Devil's half acre. This expression is also the name of a hill in Albert County.

Dick – Penis, also pecker.

Dick head – Not too bright.

Diddling – Singing a song without using words, i.e., scat singing.

Diddly squat – Almost nothing, close to worthless.

Didjaeet? – Have you eaten yet?

Digby chicken – Salt herring.

Digdeguash – Charlotte County river that flows into the Bay of Fundy.

Dinner – Noon lunch.

Dinnered out – Cookout over an open fire.

The Dip – Restaurant on Woodstock Road in Fredericton where politicians and business types were known to gather away from the downtown spotlight during the 1960s and 1970s.

Dipper Harbour – Once known as Duck Harbour and named for a duck species called dipper or bufflehead.

Disappointment Lake – Charlotte County lake that feeds the Lepreau River.

Dish the dirt – Tell the dirty gossip.

Dizzy – Not making sense. Tizzy is more of a nervous condition.

Do a McKenna – Great sales job. Frank McKenna was one of New Brunswick's best salesmen, attracting many new businesses to the province during his tenure as premier from 1987-1997. (See also 1-800-McKenna)

Doe-shay's Island – Dochet's Island in the St. Croix River, now more commonly known as St. Croix Island. The island was the site of the first winter settlement in Acadia in 1604, but the name Dochet is not traceable to a French settler. According to Stuart Trueman in *An Intimate History of New Brunswick*, "Dosia" was the nickname of Theodosia Milberry, daughter of a local clergyman, who was well-known in the community for spending time on the island with her boyfriends.

Dog-bark mariners – Navigators steering the old river boats on the St. John River reportedly steered a course at night by listening for dog barks. When they would hear a dog bark, they would move the vessel a couple of points in order to avoid ramming it up onto the shore.

Dominion of Canada – Samuel Leonard Tilley (1818-1896) coined this phrase during the Confederation era. Tilley was very religious and knew his Bible well, including a verse in Psalm Seventy-two that reads: "He shall have dominion also from sea to sea." Tilley, twice premier of New Brunswick, attended all three Confederation conferences in Charlottetown, Quebec, and London.

Donne-moi un beer, là – French-English slang for "Give me a beer."

Don't get your knickers in a twist – Don't get worked up.

Don't pay another attention to it – Pay no mind.

Do Ré Mi Bed and Breakfast – A bed and breakfast in Shediac. The house was built in 1912 as a summer home for Nova Scotia senator John McDonald and his family. McDonald built pianos, therefore the name Do Ré Mi.

Double-bitter – Double-sided axe.

Down-I-lay-me's – Bedtime prayers.

Downriver – Below where you are.

Drailing – Old fishing expression from the Grand Manan area. A boat would slowly pass over shallow shoals while a lure would be pulled through the water, attracting the fish to bite.

Drawing pogie – Unemployment insurance, now called employment insurance. Also spelled pogey or pogy.

Dressed to kill – Really dressed up.

Driv'er – Give it full speed.

Drive you around the bend – Frustration.

Drop over – Come over for a visit and don't bother to call ahead.

Droppings – Those lumps of manure found on the forest floor. Could be from a rabbit, deer, bear, or perhaps a moose. And at approximately 380 nuggets per day, a moose leaves a lot of droppings in the woods.

Drove the river – Lumber drive down the logging river by raftsmen with logs being floated all the way to the lumber mill.

Drummers – Old expression for door-to-door travelling salesmen, possibly because they were out to drum up business.

Drunk as a skunk – Stinking, falling-down drunk.

Dryfly Ramsey – Fascinating character who, along with Shadrack Nash, is a creation of mythic rural New Brunswick life in Herb Curtis's classic novel *The Americans Are*

Coming. The novel is part of *The Brennan Siding Triology* along with *The Last Tasmanian* and *The Lone Angler*.

Due bills – Instead of cash, due bills were issued to lumbermen as credits to purchase goods in company stores – goods that were often priced outrageously high.

Dulsin' and winklin' – Gathering dulse (purplish and somewhat leathery edible seaweed) and periwinkles (marine snails) around the Bay of Fundy.

Dungarvon Whooper – Whooping ghost on the Dungarvon River popularized in song by the Poet of the Renous, Michael Whelan (1858-1937). Each verse of the famous song ends with the phrase "Where the dark and deep Dungarvon sweeps along." The ghost was reputed to be that of a murdered cook and Rev. Edward Murdock, the Renous parish priest, once exorcised the evil spirit. A train running between Newcastle and Fredericton was once named the Whooper.

Dunnage – Camping gear that fits neatly in a canoe.

Dust up – Argument or fight.

Dyed-in-the-wool – Long-established and committed to the cause.

Dysart stays still better days – Liberal Premier A.A. Dysart's 1939 campaign slogan that was not well received, especially after many signs had the last two words crossed out by his political rivals.

E

Eat your porridge – During the Great Depression of the 1930s, many New Brunswick families lived on porridge and brown bread.

Eddies – Small rapids or fast-moving churns of water.

Elephant Never Forgets – How About You? – Campaign slogan of Elsie Wayne for Saint John mayor during the 1983 civic election. The slogan was designed to highlight some costly blunders of the previous administration. The "elephant ads" were effective and Elsie Wayne was voted into office, where she remained until 1993 when she successfully ran as a Progressive Conservative candidate in the federal election. The very popular Wayne was affectionately nicknamed "the old grey mayor" by Saint Johners.

The Enclosure – Historic park, cemetery, and old church site on the Miramichi River opposite Beaubears Island.

Enjoy-tu la show? – French-English slang for "Did you enjoy the show?"

Equal Opportunity – A massive social reform program during the 1960s under Louis Robichaud's Liberal government. Robichaud (1925-2005) was premier from 1960 to 1970. (See also Little Louis and Robbing Peter to pay Pierre)

Escuminac – Northumberland Strait community that is situated at the southern entrance to Miramichi Bay. From the Mi'kmaq, meaning "outlook site."

F

February with much snow, a fine summer doth foreshow – Weather foretelling.

Feed a flu, starve a cold – Old wives' tale about dealing with what ails you.

Feeling no pain – About half-way to drunk.

Fiddlehead – Delicious fern that appears in May after the flood waters recede along the rivers and streams. Also, the oldest literary magazine in Canada. Established in 1945, the literary *Fiddlehead* is published quarterly.

The Fighting Fisherman – Yvon Durelle from Bay Ste. Anne, who almost beat Archie Moore for the light-heavyweight championship of the world in a 1958 fight. The match was called "the fight of the decade" and then "the fight of the half-century." Durelle was inducted into the Boxing Hall of Fame in 1989.

Fire and brimstone – Fundamentalist expression for vibrant description of eternal punishment in hell.

Fisha – Gourmet seafood pizza at Au P'tit Mousse Restaurant in Lamèque.

Fish Fluke Point – The site of one of Grand Manan's early lighthouses at Grand Harbour.

Fish trains – Secret World War I trains that were officially called fish trains and travelled through New Brunswick on the Intercolonial Railway line carrying huge amounts of gold for the Allied war effort. "Silk trains" were also special trains that carried Chinese migrants from British Columbia to Halifax to take part in the overseas conflict.

Five Fingers – Inland community of Restigouche County that takes its name from Five Fingers Brook, which indeed has five branches.

Five Saints – Southern New Brunswick's five Saints are the communities of St. Martins, Saint John, St. George, St. Andrews, and St. Stephen.

Flat – Big case of twenty-four beer, while twelve is a carton and a six-pack a dinky.

Flatlands – Low-lying place on the Restigouche River.

Floating bog – Lumbermen dreaded having to drive logs through a floating bog where the surface was too liquid and mushy to work on.

Flood talk – From mid-March until mid-May, the topic of most conversations along the St. John River and many points inland.

Fluidly bi – English New Brunswickers who are drunk and determined to prove they are bilingual by attempting to speak French.

Fly beer – Home brew that had been set out in open kegs to ferment. Flies and other debris would make their home in the brew.

Fly grease – Any contrivance or concoction that worked to keep insects off the skin. Woodsmen went to great lengths to keep the stuff on the skin and would argue about secret formulas usually involving grease. In *Songs of Miramichi*, Louise Manny and James Reginald Wilson tell the story of Tommy Munn, who loved alcohol too much and mistook "a can of shoe polish for fly grease."

Fly Tent Brook – Stream in Northumberland County.

Fool-a-palooza – Annual April Fool's spoof concocted each year in Saint John. Spoofs and jokes are popular in the port city and one of the most memorable was the Star Buck Valley Hoax, collected from Wally Short by New Brunswick's giant storyteller, David Goss. David writes, "In the days when CFBC Radio used to carry regular Sunday morning ski reports they began getting calls from an observer at Star Buck Valley, who would report that conditions were good at Star Buck Valley even on the days when the old Rockwood Park Ski Hill would be closed to use. The announcer, who was not a ski enthusiast, accepted the reports without question, and would indicate Rockwood Park, Poley Mountain etc. are closed but conditions are good at Star Buck Valley. After a few such calls the public began to question where Star Buck Valley was, and on the next occasion when the observer called in, the announcer asked about the location. The caller, who turned out to be Cecil Dark, indicated Star Buck Valley was the cliff face near the old incinerator at the up-river end of the Reversing Falls. Of course, anyone who knew the area realized to ski down Star Buck Valley would be suicidal, and the joke was on CFBC, which at the time was the leading radio station in the city and prided itself on being both accurate and first with the news."

Fooling around – Fooling around on someone means cheating on that person.

Foot of King or Head of King – King Street in Saint John is an interesting street according to Saint Johner David Goss, who writes, "If you want to meet someone in Saint John, you might be told to rendezvous at the Foot of King. That would mean you would go to the area of Market Square, near the Market Slip where the Loyalists landed and founded the city in 1783, and perhaps stand by the Hooper Timepiece, and wait for your buddy to arrive. If you agreed to meet at the Head of King, you'd wait by the Royal Bank or the Bargain Giant store at the corner of King and Charlotte. If you were at the Foot of King, and your party did not show up, and you thought perhaps the Head of King was the meeting place, you would have to walk the equivalent of eight stories up King Street, to the Head of King. In doing so, you would have walked what Saint Johners claim is the shortest, steepest, widest main street in all Canada. It is also said Saint John women have the shapeliest legs in Canada because of this and other hills in the port city."

For a rainy day – Putting something aside for when it is needed later.

For a wet bed, eat pumpkin seeds – Cure for bed-wetting but according to humorist Stuart Trueman, one couldn't be entirely sure if this prescription would ensure a wet bed or cure you.

For cripe's sake – Swearing: for Christ's sake.

For crying out loud – That's a surprise.

Forerunners – Strange signs that seems to forecast the future.

Forest City – No city in Forest City. Just a tiny place on the Chiputneticook Lakes between New Brunswick and Maine.

For King and Country – World War I recruiting slogan.

Fort Folly Point – Tip of land in Westmorland County that juts into Shepody Bay. According to place name expert Alan Rayburn, tidal surges around the upper Fundy Bay placed early mariners in considerable danger and is one plausible explanation for this unique place name.

Forty-Five River – Flows into the Salmon River in Fundy National Park above Alma at a forty-five-degree angle.

Foxes in the henhouse – A conflict of interest.

Fredericopolis silvae filia nobilis – Frederiction city motto: Fredericton, noble daughter of the forest.

Free pour – Open bar, i.e., when drinks are on the house.

Freshets – Spring flash flooding usually caused by ice jams or fast-melting snow upriver.

Friars Head – Rocky point on Campobello Island that has been described as resembling a friar's cropped head of hair.

Fricot – Hearty Acadian soup that contains potatoes, meat or fish and usually includes dumplings, also known as poutines.

Friggit – To heck with it.

Frolic – In olden times, frolics were community socials and cooperative work events that were used for barn-raising efforts and home-building, as well as for plowing, planting, and other labour-demanding chores. Neighbours would bring their horses or oxen, and tools, as well as plenty of food and drink, and the day would be spent working while the evening would be a celebration of food, drink, and good cheer.

Frost on the pumpkin – Ideal time, when great things can happen.

Frosty Hollow – Dip of land on Route 106 outside of Sackville that reportedly has the first frost each fall.

Frye Festival – Not a fried food festival but the Northrop Frye Literary Festival in Moncton, named in honour of the province's famous literary critic. Frye (1912-1991) was one of the leading literary critics and theorists of the twentieth century.

Full of beans – Less than truthful and full of exaggeration.

Full of lead – Slow, as in "Get the lead out and get going!"

Full-stretched – Lord Beaverbrook's expression for being stressed out. (See also The Beaver)

G

Ga'day – Good day.

Gallivanting – Carefree and not very reliable.

Gawgaw – Young man with little common sense.

Gawkin' – Nosey busybody, a gawker does not mind his or her own business.

Geary – Sunbury County community that was once called New Niagara since the early settlers were United Empire Loyalists from the Niagara region. Some nineteenth-century maps spell it Gary. According to William Hamilton in his *Place Names of Atlantic Canada*, Geary was derived from the local pronunciation of Niagara (Ni-a-ga-ree.)

Geezer – Old guy.

Get nookie – Have sexual intercourse.

Getter – Guitar, also known as the get-box.

Getting away with murder – Not getting caught or reprimanded for an offence.

Getting on the outside – Close to the end, as in getting on the outside of a bottle of whisky.

Getting too big for your britches – Attempting to go

above your station in life, as in being too ambitious or demanding.

Getting ugly – Dispute is getting serious. Ugly is angry, as in "She was some ugly."

Getting your dandruff up – Getting riled up over something.

Getting your skin – Sexual intercourse.

Get up off your high horse – Don't be so high and mighty.

Get wigged – Miramichi phrase meaning to get robbed.

Gift of the gab – Can sure talk.

Gillie – Old term for fishing guide that originated in Scotland as ghillie.

Gin Creek – Small stream with water of an unusual colour that flows into the Kedgwick River near the Quebec border.

Girl who rouges – Wears lipstick.

Give me a slug – Give me a drink.

Give us the word, we'll run the rum in – Famous line from "The Smugglers' Chanty," a folksong sung by liquor smugglers off Kent County in the 1920s.

Gleaner – *The Daily Gleaner*, Fredericton's daily newspaper, which started in 1880.

Glooscap Reach – Section of the Mactaquac Headpond in York County that, according to Aboriginal oral tradition, once belonged to the legendary Mi'kmaq and Maliseet god named Glooscap.

Going right at it – Getting it done as quickly as possible.

Going to the john – Washroom.

Going to town – Leaving the house.

Golden Age – Before Confederation (1867) and the founding of Canada when we think the Maritimes really had it going.

Golden Ball – K.C. Irving's original five-storey building in Saint John. Named after the unique orb that dangled in front. (See also Man from Bouctouche and K.C.)

Golden Mile – Moncton's St. George Boulevard, where many international companies established east coast branches in the 1960s. Civic leaders called the street "the golden mile" because of the additional property taxes that flowed into the city.

Good head – Good person. Also, a good egg.

Good head on his shoulders – Smart person.

Good kick in the ass – Tried most everything, last resort is a good kick . . . Also, a good lickin'.

Good Roads Veniot – Nickname for the first Acadian premier, Liberal Peter J. Veniot. He employed thousands of party supporters to build the first major system of highways in the province. Veniot (1863-1936) was premier from 1923 to 1925. Long a force in New Brunswick politics, he retained his influence even after his election to the federal House of Commons in 1926.

Goose tongue greens – Edible green (passe-pierre in French) that is found on the muddy banks of the Petitcodiac River and other tidal sites along the Bay of Fundy.

Gorby – Greedy or lacking in manners. The term comes from the lumber camps, where loggers nicknamed the noisy and greedy Grey Jay bird "gorby."

Gormans Gulch – Wilderness ravine in Gloucester County.

Gorney – Rusagonis, Sunbury County community near Sunpoke Lake.

Got 'er made – Living on easy street without having to work hard.

Got his papers – Finished the course.

Got my stamps – Enough eligibility to start collecting pogie. A reference to the days when the government unemployment insurance program issued stamps for each week of employment. (See also Drawing pogie)

Got the brains – The smart one.

Got the guts – Brave, having the courage to do it.

Got to see a man about a horse – Time to exit for the washroom.

Government Open Water – Stretch of the Restigouche River reserved for salmon fishing by New Brunswickers, as most of the river's fishing sites are leased to the highest bidder.

Grand-Anse – A coastal Gloucester County community. Grand-Anse is a descriptive Acadian name for a small cove along the shore.

Grand-Digue – A community on Shediac Bay whose descriptive French name means "dyke."

Granite town – Town of St. George that became famous for its red granite building stone, running from deep red to light pink and sold under the trade name St. George Red.

Grassin' – Making out in the field, as in "We went grassin' on Baker Hill."

Greased – Bought off or bribed.

Greased line – Old-time fly-fishing line that would stay up on top of the water better after it was rubbed down. This process was called greasing a line but mainly involved removing the water from the line.

Greaser – Cook in a lumber camp.

Greatest fire of all time – The Great Miramichi Fire of 1825 that destroyed one-fifth of the entire province. After a severe lengthy summer drought, the largest fire of all time in eastern North America began October 7, 1825. Fanned by strong winds, fires raged through a rough triangle stretching from Beldune to Richibucto to an apex near Fredericton.

Greatest little city in the east – Mayor Elsie Wayne's description of Saint John, also called the best little city "east of Montreal."

The Green – Riverfront park in Fredericton near the Beaverbrook Art Gallery. (See also Waterloo Row)

Grey big – Quite big.

Grilse – Young salmon and a smolt is a younger salmon. A parr is a very young salmon.

Gros Tyme – Summertime Wednesday night Acadian musical party at Le Pays de la Sagouine in Bouctouche. (See also Pays de la Sagouine and La Sagouine)

Grub – Food. Grub Road is in Albert County near River Glade.

Gulch – Ravine.

Gutta hav' it – Must have it.

Guzzle it – Drink or eat it quickly.

Gyles Cove – Place in York County that was named after John Gyles, a legendary New Brunswicker who was captured as a young boy by Aboriginal warriors in 1689 and spent six years among the Maliseet. Gyles later wrote a vivid and gripping account that was published in 1736 and reissued in 1966 as *The Ordeal of John Gyles*.

H

Hackmatack – Fast-growing evergreen tree that is unique among native conifers in shedding its foliage each year. Known as juniper or larch outside the Maritimes.

Hacky – Hockey.

Had the biscuit – Tired from all the activity.

Ha Ha Cemetery – Cemetery in Albert County on Route 915 near Shepody.

Hair of the dog – The morning-after drink of the alcoholic beverage that was consumed in large quantities the night before.

Half cut – Only about fifty percent drunk.

Hang up – Abnormal fixation but in New Brunswick, the term also had a meaning in the timber trade. Hang ups were logs snagged on a waterfall or rapids.

Happy as a clam – Satisfied.

Harbour Station – Exhibition and all-purpose centre in Saint John.

Hard on – An erection.

Hardscrabble No. 2 Covered Bridge – Beautiful New

Brunswick icon near St. Martins. There were once more than one hundred wooden bridges in the province and now there are about seventy-four still standing.

Hard stuff – Hard liquor, drugs, etc.

Hard ticket – Tough guy.

Hard up – In tough shape, bleak prospects.

Hatfield Potato Chips – Old brand of New Brunswick's very own potato chips once produced in Hartland by the family of the late Premier Richard Hatfield.

Haven't got a hope or a prayer – Not much chance it will happen.

Haven't got a pot to piss in – Really poor.

Haven't seen you in a dog's age – A long time.

Hawkshaw – On the St. John River near Nackawic in York County. Named after nineteenth-century business leader Howard Shaw, who was nicknamed "Hawk."

Heathenish notions – Devilish ideas, i.e., bad.

Hellifax – Halifax, Nova Scotia.

Hell knoweth no fury like a politician scorned – Veteran political figure R.A. Tweedie's observation on politicians' wrath when they are unhappy. Tweedie worked for twenty-five years (1935-60) as New Brunswick's key civil servant and was closely associated with three provincial premiers.

Hello fer going! – Going flat out.

Hell's Kitchen – Steep ravine in Fundy National Park.

Herring chokers – Bay of Fundy fishermen.

Herring horse – Bay of Fundy term for a large stick containing many herring that two men would carry to the smokehouse to dry and smoke. Men putting the herring on the stick are called herring stringers.

He's a real pill – Handfull, as in hard to keep under control.

Hickey – Red spot on the skin from kissing while a dewhickey is a private body part, usually male genitalia.

Hicktown – Backwards place.

Highfalutin – Putting on airs, being pretentious.

High on the hog – Living beyond your means, as in spending more than you are earning.

Highsawvah – French-English slang, Hi, ça va, meaning "Hi, how are you?"

Hither and yon – From far and wide.

Hodge podge – First big mess of new vegetables made up of new potatoes, carrots, peas and beans, butter and milk (all essential) and whatever else you can add.

Hogged – Nautical term that may have come from the classic Mi'kmaq canoe design that featured a "hogged" centre, each side curved upward in the middle in order to remain stable in open water.

Hog it all – Being a pig about it and taking more than your fair share.

Hogshead – Wooden cask containing at least sixty gallons of liquid.

Hole-in-the-Wall – Rock formation on the North Head

shore of Grand Manan Island that features a large see-through hole in the cliff.

Holy cow – What a surprise.

Home of the Enterprise Range – Old marketing slogan that stood for years across the Enterprise Foundry building in Sackville, promoting one of the best-known stoves in Canada. For many years, the Enterprise had one main challenger for dominance in the Canadian stove business and that was a crosstown rival, the popular Fawcett stove. In 1982 Enterprise went into receivership and its assets were sold to Enheat Inc. of Sackville, owners of Fawcett. Enterprise Fawcett Ltd. still manufactures cookstoves, heaters, and furnaces.

Home of the Silver Fox – Salisbury, where Fred Colpitts developed a large fox breeding business in the early 1900s.

Home pool – Salmon pool on the Upsalquitch River that was "a good producer" according to George Frederick Clarke. Also, the name of a book by Philip Lee about the fight to save the Atlantic salmon.

Honest to Jesus and Murphy – Pledge it's true to all concerned.

Honking – Throwing up due to too much to drink.

Hooper Timepiece – Large working clock in Saint John's Market Square district. This icon of the city was produced by sculptor John Hooper of Hampton and Jack Massey, a chair-maker from Darlings Island.

Hoosegow – Jail, in the clink.

Hootch – Moonshine, so a hootch-maker would be an operator of a still.

Hopewell Cape – Albert County community that juts out into the lower Petitcodiac River neat Shepody Bay. The name can be traced to Hopewell, Pennsylvania. In the 1760s, a group of German-speaking immigrants left the region for the Petitcodiac, where they established a township at Hopewell.

Horse of a different colour – A whole new topic.

Horsepower – Old unit of measurement that was equivalent to 33,000 foot-pounds of work per minute.

How's your hammer hanging? – How are you?

How the wind blows – That's the nature of it and there's not much we can do about it.

How ya makiner? – How are you doing?

The Hub – Moncton, geographical centre of the Maritimes.

Hue and Cry – Old-time street sign that warned citizens about escaped criminals on the loose. Proclamation would be entitled "hue and cry."

Humdergeon – Good worker with lots of get up and go.

Humdinger – Finest kind, as in a humdinger of a story.

Hummed and hawed – Can't make a decision.

Humphrey woolens – Durable woolen pants made by Humphrey Mills in Moncton, beginning in the 1880s.

Hump Yard – CN's (Canadian National) boxcar centre on the outskirts of Moncton, where trains are shunted around. Some trains carry signs that say "Do Not Hump."

I

I could tell worse than that – A terrible story could be told.

If you want more dances vote for Francis – Frank McKenna's 1965 campaign slogan for school president, Grade 12, Sussex High School. McKenna eventually became premier of the province. (See also 1-800-McKenna)

I like to see wheels turning – K.C. Irving's explanation for his enduring business drive. (See also K.C. and Man from Bouctouche)

In a blue moon – It will never happen.

In a pig's eye – Not very likely to happen.

In a snit – Uptight.

In cahoots – Forming an alliance or secret partnership.

Inch Arran Point – Along the Baie des Chaleurs in Restigouche County. The name derives from an early settler, John Hamilton, who came from Arran, Scotland. Inch is also Scottish in origin and is often used to describe a small piece of land.

Inneresting – Interesting.

In one ear and out the other – Not listening.

In politics, you can't take any chances – Richard Hatfield's political philosophy. Hatfield (1931-1991) served as premier from 1970 to 1987. Both revered and reviled, the colourful Hatfield was a player in national politics with an important role in the patriation of the Canadian Constitution and the Charter of Rights and Freedoms in 1982.

Inside Connection – Aboveground, indoor pedway system, Uptown Saint John.

Intervale – Fertile lowland along a river that gets flooded most spring seasons and produces good quality hay. There are twelve intervale names throughout New Brunswick.

In the velvet – A moose whose antlers are covered in a mossy soft substance nicknamed velvet.

Island – Prince Edward Island.

It was no do – It wasn't a fun event, as opposed to a "real do" that was exciting.

J

Jacking – Hunting at night with a light.

Jack of all trades – Many talents or hobbies but can also mean stretched too thin, as in jack of all trades but master of none.

Jakey – Old name for lemon extract that was shipped into New Brunswick in long-necked bottles during Prohibition in the 1920s and '30s to serve as a liquor substitute.

Jamaica – Rum in the keg from the West Indies.

Jemseg – From the Maliseet, Ah-jim-sek, and loosely translated as a storage or depot site since the location close to Grand Lake and the St. John River meant that the Maliseet could store supplies there and pick them up before travelling up into Grand Lake or back to the St. John.

Jesiless – Cursing, as in "This jesiless thing!"

Jigging – Trying to hook a fish by dropping a lure over its back and pulling up.

Jig was up – Originally, the musical reel was over but became an equivalent phrase for describing the end of virtually any operation.

Joe Walnut – The "King of Madawaska" during the 1920s and the biggest bootlegger to ever operate in the Maritimes. His real name was Albenie J. Violette and he managed to outsmart and intimidate the authorities for a decade. And during that decade, King Walnut had a Robin Hood-like reputation along the St. John River.

Johnny Woodboat – The St. John River woodboat was unique to the lower St. John and was primarily used as a wood carrier. Up until Confederation, the vessel was unequalled as a cargo carrier. It was a snub-nosed little vessel with a flat bottom and bilge keel to permit it to stand upright when left dry by the ebb of the Bay of Fundy tides.

Joie de vivre – Vibrant Acadian spirit and joy of living.

Jolicure – Westmorland County community near the Nova Scotia border. Name derives from an early Acadian family.

Jolstay – Bay of Fundy expression meaning "golly" or "my goodness."

Jumping through hoops – Unnecessary holdups or delays.

Just enough fog to keep it cold – Weather in Saint John and most of the Bay of Fundy coast.

Just putting you on – Teasing.

Just spinning your wheels – Going nowhere.

K

K.C. – Kenneth Colin Irving, the biggest entrepreneur and business operator New Brunswick ever knew. Irving (1899-1992) founded an empire that includes forest products, an oil refinery, gas stations, trucking, newspaper publishing, and broadcasting.

Keel over – Nautical in origin but expression means falling-down drunk.

Keep the home fires burning – Please keep the place warm while we are away.

Kennebecasis River – Kings County river that starts in Westmorland County and flows into Kennebecasis Bay and on to the St. John River. According to Alan Rayburn, the word is from the Maliseet Kennepekachichk and means "little long bay place," but storyteller David Goss thinks he knows the real story. When two brothers named Casey became separated while fishing on a foggy night, one kept calling out to the other brother, "Can it be Case's?"

Kennebecker – Carrying bag used to store belongings when travelling into lumber camps. Maine's Kennebec River lumber boys were the first to have these bags when they arrived at the camps.

Kerfuffle – Dispute.

Keswick – York County community. Also a river that flows into the St. John River. From the Maliseet (Kookumkeech) that, according to William Ganong, can be translated as a rocky or gravelly river.

Keyhole – Narrow section of the Point Wolfe River in Fundy Park that used to be a nightmare for lumberjacks driving logs down the river.

Kicked the bucket – Died.

Killoween – Carleton County community near Bath. Named for Charles Russell, Baron Russell of Killowen, a nineteenth-century British statesman.

Kingsclear – York County community above Fredericton that was named in recognition of the King's eighteenth-century right to grant cutting rights on all property only after the prized tall white pine trees were taken for constructing masts on his naval vessels.

Kipperin' – Smoking fish in a smokehouse. All sorts of fish, including salmon, would be smoked but herring was and is the most popular. Smoked herring would be hung in "bays" up to three weeks over a spruce sawdust fire before the rich taste of the spruce smoke could be fully absorbed into the fish. The person in charge of a smokehouse is called the smoke tender. At Cap-Pelé, there are thirty commercial smokehouses producing smoked herring.

Kishimaquac or Kouchibouguac – Also called "Kouchy." Kent County river and bay on the Northumberland Strait and now a national park. From the Mi'kmaq Pijeboogwek, meaning "river of the long tideway."

Kiss her cheeks and chin – Traditional greeting for a bride.

Knee – Piece of wood with a natural bend that could be adapted to fit into an angle or corner to function as a brace to support a structure. Old shipbuilders, as well as home and barn carpenters, often used knees to escape having to build support beams from scratch.

Knee-high to a grasshopper – A very young person.

L

La Fête – La Fête nationale des Acadiens – Acadian Day, August 15.

Laird of Shediac – Historian John Clarence Webster (1863-1950), a founder of the New Brunswick Museum. A pioneer surgeon in obstetrics and gynecology working in Edinburgh, Montreal, and Chicago, he returned to Shediac in 1919 and turned his attention to history.

Lake Utopia – This body of water in Charlotte County came about its name in a rather unusual manner. At the end of the Revolutionary War, members of the Royal Fencible Americans were granted farmland but when they complained to Governor Carleton that the lands were underwater, he named the lake Utopia – "a land of abundance and perfection, but entirely ideal."

Lamb's quarters – Delicious wild green found along Fundy Bay and tasting somewhere between swiss chard and spinach.

Lampers – Lamprey eels that come upriver at certain times of the year.

Larrigans – Heavy waterproof leather moccasins or boots that were usually ankle length but could go as high up as the knee. During the late nineteenth century, the Eaton &

Armstrong Moccasin Factory near St. Stephen turned out great numbers of larrigans.

Larry's Gulch – Famous old salmon pool and lodge on the Restigouche River now owned by the provincial government and used as a fishing camp for officials and government guests.

La Sagouine – Fictional Acadian scrubwoman created by noted writer Antonine Maillet. La Sagouine is the Acadian voice of hardship, courage, and pride. Maillet wrote *La Sagouine* in 1971 and it was translated into English in 1979. In 1979 the native of Bouctouche won France's premier literary prize, the Prix Concourt, for *Pélagie la Charrette*, a mythic account of the Acadian Deportation. (See also Gros Tyme and Pays de la Sagouine)

Lead team – The best pair of horses in a lumber camp.

Less than a full deck – A person with not all faculties in full working order.

Let's Clean House – Tory 1952 campaign slogan that featured editorial commentaries placed in newspapers as advertising pieces written by Dalton Camp and signed L.C. House. The well-orchestrated campaign ended with the election of a Conservative provincial government under Hugh John Flemming.

Let's side up – Straighten up and do a light cleaning, as in "Let's side up the camp before we go."

Lightning seeks water – Advice to remember when a lightning storm is approaching.

Lights are on but no one is home – Person is not getting the picture.

Like a steel-trap door – Sharp mind that picks up on everything.

Line-house – Prohibition-era name for homes along the Maine-New Brunswick border that were situated on the actual boundary line. They were usually full of booze. American Prohibition was declared prior to Canada going dry and during this period, virtually all boundary or line-houses bootlegged liquor into the U.S.

Little boy's room – Washroom.

Little bugger – Calling a person down, whereas "poor little bugger" is feeling sorry for the person.

Little Louis – Louis J. Robichaud (1925-2005) was one of New Brunswick's more controversial and important political figures, reorganizing the province's social structure in the 1960s. (See also Equal Opportunity and Robbing Peter to pay Pierre)

Little North Pole – Northumberland County stream.

Little nude dude – Nickname for Freddie the Fountain on Queen Street in front of Fredericton City Hall.

Loaded – Rich, weighted down, or having consumed too much alcohol.

Lobster Capital of the World – Shediac, where an annual lobster festival goes back over fifty years. Today, the community features a giant lobster at the entrance to town.

Local boy makes good – Referencing young men who have left the province and made a fortune elsewhere.

Loco – Steam locomotive, also known as a smoker and a pig.

Long in the tooth – Getting old.

Look what the cat drug in – Ironic and playful greeting that may have had its origins on the Miramichi.

Lost cos – Nickname for Cosmopolitan Club in Moncton (and previously in Fredericton) since finding a suitable date at the Cos often proved to be a lost cause.

Loyalist City – Saint John. Named in 1785 and proclaimed a city complete with a royal charter, the first incorporated city in Canada.

LRs – Low rentals.

Luxuriating – High living in a luxurious manner.

M

Mackenaw – Woolen coat that originated in Wisconsin and was popular in the lumber industry.

Mackerel sky is not long dry – Old fisherman saying for predicting rain.

Madawaska – River and county in the northwestern part of the province that can be traced to the Maliseet Medaweskak, which has been translated as "where one river enters another" by Silas Rand and "land of porcupines" by William Hamilton and Alan Rayburn.

Madawaska Weaver – Nickname for Conservative leader Bernard Valcourt, coined by Liberal cabinet minister Ray Frenette. Valcourt was from Madawaska County, and Frank McKenna's Liberals were able to discredit his campaign and went on to win the 1995 provincial election.

Made a tidy pile – Socked the money away.

Made it up out of clear wool – Real fiction.

Magga-dave-ick – Magaguadavic. Also called "Mac-a-day-vy" by William Ganong. Lake and river in York and Charlotte Counties that has been traced to the Maliseet (or Passamaquoddy) Mageecaatawik that means "river of big eels."

Main John – The boss of an operation but the term is derived from an old New Brunswick lumber camp where a giant of a man, lumber baron John Glasier (1809-1894), ruled the woods with an iron fist. When Glasier entered politics, he introduced himself in the New Brunswick Legislature as "John Glasier, the Main John!" (See also Walking boss)

Making out – Lovemaking.

Makings – Roll your own cigarettes. Store-bought are tailor-made.

Making the rounds – Visiting everyone in town.

Malabeam – Mythic Maliseet maiden who was taken prisoner by Mohawk warriors on the upper St. John River and saved her people by leading the war party down the river in canoes and to their demise over the rocky gorge at Grand Falls.

Maliseet – First Nation people, sometimes called Malecite or Wolastoqiyik, who are situated in six communities along the St. John River and its tributaries.

Man behind the plow – The guy who works the hardest.

Man from Bouctouche – K.C. Irving. (See also K.C.)

Man who controls the temperature in Moncton – Old Captain J.E. Masters, who ran a coal supply business as well as an ice operation in the city prior to World War I.

Marco Polo – The legendary three-masted, square-rigged sailing vessel built in Saint John by James Smith in 1851 which set a sailing record from Liverpool, England, to Australia and back in 1852. In 1883 the ship wrecked at Cavendish, Prince Edward Island.

Market Slip – A slip is an opening between wharfs in a harbour where vessels can come right up to the shore. Market Slip in Saint John harbour is one of the oldest and most historic sites in New Brunswick. During the American Revolution, the Loyalists landed there in 1783. Throughout the nineteenth century, vessels came to Market Slip loaded with produce that could be sold at the nearby city market.

Mat rags – Green pole beans that are mature and hung to dry on strings behind a wood stove.

May run – Not the first salmon run but the very important Victoria Day party weekend when campgrounds traditionally open and everyone gets drunk in front of an open fire.

McCain's – The largest producer of frozen French fries in the world is based in Florenceville.

Meat and potatoes – Basic, no frills or fancy stuff.

Mechanic Settlement – Kings County community that was established by Saint John labourers in the 1840s.

Mecklenburg Street – Hard to spell street in Saint John, so hard in fact that according to David Goss, a poor-spelling policeman on the beat found a dead horse on Mecklenburg, knew he would have to write up a report, so dragged the dead animal one full block north and filed the report indicating that the horse had been found at Duke and Wentworth.

Medicinal purposes only – Excuse for drinking liquor that goes back to Prohibition when liquor was only legal with a doctor's prescription.

Meductic – York County settlement that has been traced to the Maliseet "Medoctic" and according to Alan Rayburn means "the end." This site on the St. John River was at the end of the historic Eel River portage route that allowed Aboriginal travellers to reach the St. John from deep within the Maine woods.

Meeting-house – Sites in early communities that served as all-purpose houses of worship, as well as political and social centres.

Memramcook – Community and river in Westmorland County. The name is derived from the Mi'kmaq Amlam-cook, which means "where the rock has varied colours."

Menagoeuche – Aboriginal word for Saint John that still survives today in some form: Manawagonish Road. Manawagonish is also the name of a cove and creek near Saint John and can be loosely translated as "place for clams."

Mending of the line – Fly-fishing phrase describing a situation when the line gets ahead of the fly on a fast current. To mend the line (get it back behind the fly) without having to recast, you lift up the rod and get the line to roll without disturbing the fly. An art that must be practised to be perfected.

Mend your ways – Better try harder.

Mennetic Hill – Magnetic Hill outside of Moncton. An optical illusion first popularized in 1933 by journalist Stuart Trueman and developed into a tourist attraction by entrepreneur Muriel Lutes. Drive your car to the bottom of the hill, stay in the car, put it in neutral and watch as the car rolls back *up* the hill without motor power.

Me pipe – My pipe, my hat, etc. Me for my.

Merimashee (Murrymashee) – Miramichi. Perhaps one of the oldest Aboriginal place names still in use in North America.

Metepenagiag – On the Miramichi River near Red Bank in Northumberland County. One of the most important Aboriginal historic sites in New Brunswick.

Mickey – The term appeared in New Brunswick during the mid-1800s and referred to a Roman Catholic, especially an Irish Catholic. Orangemen were Protestants and competed with Catholics for political and economic dominance throughout the late nineteenth century and well into the twentieth century.

Mi'kmaq – First Nation people indigenous to eastern New Brunswick, Prince Edward Island, Nova Scotia, and parts of Newfoundland, Quebec, and New England. Mi'kmaw is the singular form of Mi'kmaq. Historically, the New Brunswick land mass was shared among the Mi'kmaq, Maliseet, and Passamaquoddy First Nations.

Millinyers – Jumbled or confused words.

Millionaire's Pool – Where the Patapedia meets the Restigouche stands one of the best salmon pools in the world, where millionaires from all over the world come to fish and relax.

Million Dollar Fire – 1905 fire at the Intercolonial Railway Shops in Moncton.

Millwright – Mechanic in charge of equipment at a mill.

Minto miner's roast – Reheated bologna that was also called Albert County or Back Bay steak, and according to writer Stuart Trueman was a little less expensive than Saint John tubular steak (a wiener).

Miramichi City – Amalgamated in 1995, the city of 18,500 includes the older communities of Newcastle, Chatham, Douglastown, Loggieville, and Nelson-Miramichi.

Miramichi Folksong Festival – Begun in 1958 by Louise Manny and others to feature the oral folk traditions of the Miramichi region.

Miscou Island – The name is Mi'kmaq, derived from Susqu, which means "low bogs" or "marsh."

Missaguash River – This river forms the southern border with Nova Scotia and comes from the Mi'kmaq word for muskrat.

Mistake Cove – After travelling up the Long Reach of the St. John River, early travellers would often bear to the left, thinking they were still in the main channel. After several miles they would discover their mistake: they had reached a dead end.

Mister man – Very excited, as in "Let me tell you, mister man, I was so mad."

Molasses – Molasses is a thick and tasty liquid that is derived from the refining of sugar cane and once served as the principal sweetener in most homes throughout New Brunswick. Every Maritimer of a certain age grew up on molasses and may not have always liked it but ate it anyway. Crosby's Molasses Company was first incorporated in Saint John one hundred years ago.

Monkey town – Moncton, where Monctonians live.

Moose – Within Canada, moose is used in an official

name 662 times according to Alan Rayburn in *Naming Canada*, and the term is no less popular in New Brunswick. Originally called moose-deer by early British explorers, the term deer was later dropped.

Moose fly – A big fly that seems to drive moose crazy at certain times of the year. In fact, it is said that when flies are thick in the woods, moose are driven out onto the highways (and into cars) in order to get away from the dreaded insects.

Moosehead Beer Company – Canada's largest independently owned brewery, located in Saint John. "The Moose is loose" is their famous advertising slogan. Moosehead's roots go back to 1867 when Susannah Oland started the Army & Navy Brewery in Dartmouth, Nova Scotia.

Moosemilk – Rum and eggnog, perfect for the morning after the night before.

Morse Code Cottages – On Grand Manan Island, the cottages have a view of the Swallowtail Lighthouse. The name was selected by the original owners Roger and Joan Morse.

Mortise and tenon – Joint in the frame of a house. The mortise is the opening that receives the tenon.

Mosquito Lake – Charlotte County lake above New River.

Most wanted man – Henry More Smith, expert escape artist and nineteenth-century mystery man. In 1814 Smith was jailed in Kingston, New Brunswick, as a horse thief, but escaped twice and while in jail managed to constantly get out of leg chains, handcuffs, and neck collars. Sentenced to death, he appealed and was pardoned.

Mount A – Mount Allison University in Sackville.

Mountaineer – Two horses would often tow a timber raft upriver, one near the shore, and the other horse was the mountaineer since it walked on higher ground well above the shoreline.

Muckraking – Used in politics to refer to digging up the dirt on someone, as in raking around in the muck.

Mucky mucks – Very important persons.

Mullins Boom – Northumberland County jail. A boom was a floating chain of logs fastened together to confine the logs and thus a person could also be confined. Mullins was the jailer of Miramichi County. The Kent County jail at Rexton was called Mooney's Boom.

Mutchklins – Historic measure for wine that originated in Scotland.

N

Nackawic – Community and stream in York County on the St. John River. Name is Maliseet derived and comes from Nelgwaweegek that has been translated as "straight stream."

Napadogan – Community, lake and brook in northern York County that is Maliseet in origin. Napudaagun means "brook to be followed" and may have meant that the brook could lead a traveller into the Miramichi Lake and on to the Miramichi River.

Nashwaakers – Someone from the Naskwaak River Valley. Naskwaak is derived from the Maliseet Nahwijewauk.

Nashwaaksis – Community and stream now part of the city of Fredericton. The word is Maliseet in origin and means "Little Naskwaak."

Needle dick – Tall, slim person.

Neg-oo-wack – Neguac in Gloucester County. Mi'kmaq name that can be traced to Negwek and translates as "springs out of the ground."

Nepisiquit – River, falls, lake, and bay are located on the north shore and the name can be traced to the Mi'kmaq word Winpegijawik, which means "rough water."

Never go to bed with cold feet – Nineteenth-century advice for staying healthy.

Never sleep in a draught – Good advice for avoiding colds.

New Brunswick is where the good canoe cedar grows – Chestnut Canoe Company's old advertising slogan. Henry and Harry Chestnut got a patent in 1905 for a wood and canvas canoe, and eventually expanded to fifty different models. The company closed in 1979 and the canoe forms dispersed. *The Story of the Chestnut Canoe* by Kenneth Solway is the biography of the fabled craft. (See also Ogilvy Special)

New Canaan – United Empire Loyalist Ward Chipman's proposed name for New Brunswick.

Nictau – Settlement and lake in Victoria County. The community is located at the forks of the Tobique River and comes from the Maliseet Niktawk.

Night fog in the hollow means warm tomorrow – Weather forecasting.

Nip and tuck – Just barely getting by.

No faster than a walk – Old traffic rule for crossing a covered bridge in a horse and wagon.

No flies on her – Quick and smart.

None too pleased – Not very happy.

North Esk Boom – Community on the Northwest Miramichi River near Eel Ground.

North Shore – Campbellton to the Miramichi.

No skin off my ass – Not going to hurt me.

Nothing in my head I bring, simply to my name I cling – Liberal leader Peter Veniot's bitter but apt ode to inept Conservative Premier L.P.D. Tilley during the 1935 provincial campaign. Tilley was the son of Sir Samuel L. Tilley, a Father of Confederation and New Brunswick's most important nineteenth-century political figure.

Not what he's cracked up to be – Not fulfilling his potential, disappointing.

Not worth a fiddler's dam – Hardly worth anything.

Number one go-getter – Aggressive deal closer.

Nutter Brook – Sunbury County stream near Juvenile Settlement.

O

Ocean Limited – Famous passenger train that runs through eastern New Brunswick from Halifax to Montreal. The Ocean is now operated by VIA Rail. The oldest, continuously operated, named passenger train in North America began July 3, 1904.

October snow brings want and woe – Freak weather can bring ruin.

Ogilvy Special – Famous Chestnut Canoe made in collaboration with the deans of New Brunswick wilderness guides, David and Jock Ogilvy. "Very light draft, straight on the bottom and so flat from side to side that it skims over the top of the water rather than through it." (See also New Brunswick is where the good canoe cedar grows)

Oh migawd – Oh my God.

Old clunker – Beat-up car.

Old fart – Good old friend.

Old-fashioned nor'easter – Winter storms that wreck havoc on the province.

Old King Cole – Famous tea produced by the Barbour Company. George and William Barbour founded the company in 1867. Now located in Sussex, it still produces Old

King Cole and Morse's Tea, as well as Barbour's Peanut Butter and Barbour's Spices.

Old Sow – Second largest whirlpool in the world between Deer Island and Eastport and driven by currents that flow around the island.

Old Taboo – Nickname for the Tabusintac River in Gloucester County.

On a roll – Having a bit of a lucky streak.

On easy street – Having it made by not having to work hard.

1-800-McKenna – Advertising slogan during Premier Frank McKenna's term of office (1987-97). If you were interested in setting up shop in New Brunswick, you could call McKenna directly, no waiting around.

One horse affair – Single issue and not very important.

One minute to the pound – Old fishing guide's assessment for how long the average salmon will fight before it is ready for the net or the gaff.

One-upmanship – Getting ahead of another person.

On the barrelhead – Upfront, no waiting around, as in paying cash at the time of the transaction.

On the mink – On the prowl for sex.

On the nod – Falling off to sleep.

On the take – Having been bought off or susceptible to a bribe.

On with the dance – Premier A.A. Dysart's famous saying that signals the end of a conversation according to his secretary, R.A. Tweedie, who entitled his own memoir *On With the Dance*. Albert Allison Dysart (1880-1962) was premier from 1935 to 1940.

Oromocto – Town, island, lake, and river in Sunbury County. The Maliseet name Welamootook was first given to the river and means "good river for canoe."

Other side – United States of America.

Out west – All of the Canadian provinces west of Ontario.

Oven – Coastal caves that are formed from tidal action.

Over north – Over and up, for example from Fredericton, over north to the Miramichi.

Over river – Across the river.

Over the line – The U.S.A.

Over town – Across town.

Owly – Foul mood, as in "Things didn't go well, so he was some owly."

P

Pabineau River – Gloucester County name that is derived from both the Mi'kmaq and French in that both Wosabaygul (Mi'kmaq) and pabina (French) are names given to a local cranberry bush.

Packing it in – Giving up on it.

Painsec Junction – Railway and highway crossings near Moncton.

Panther piss – After government liquor stores were established in 1927, they had trouble competing with bootleggers and in 1933 introduced a rock-bottom brand of cheap wine at sixty-five cents a quart. The intoxicant immediately caught the attention of the low-end drinkers and received a host of nicknames, including goof, bingo, sneaky Pete, and perhaps the best one: panther piss.

Pan trout – Brook trout, approximately six to eight inches long, that fit into a frying pan.

Paper boats – Newsprint carriers that pick up cargo from the paper mills at Dalhousie, Miramichi, and Saint John.

Parlee Beach – The most popular beach in the Maritimes. Near Shediac, it was known as Belliveau Beach until 1958. The tragic death of a popular Moncton-area man,

T. Babbitt Parlee, in a 1956 airplane crash induced the community to honour the name of this promising politician.

Passamaquoddy – Charlotte County body of water and the name of an Aboriginal First Nation that was derived from the word Peskutumaquadik. Passamaquoddy people were historically associated with the nearby Maliseet Nation.

Passed away – Polite way for saying so-and-so died.

Pass on the right – Slogan for motorists in 1922 when New Brunswick changed over to driving on the right side of the road. At the time Nova Scotia was still driving on the opposite side and a newspaper editorial advised: "Drive slow you may meet a fool and of course, a fool may meet a fool."

Patience of Job – Biblical reference to Job, who had lots of patience.

Patriotic potato gift – A simple attempt to send potatoes from the people of New Brunswick to the people of Great Britain during World War I turned into a boondoggle involving an overspent budget, rotten potatoes, kickbacks, and payoffs.

Pays de la Sagouine – Bouctouche theme park centred around the mythical Acadian character La Sagouine. (See also La Sagouine)

Pea soup fog – Thick Bay of Fundy fog that blankets the region in early summer.

Peekaboo Corner – Kings County community near Norton.

Peelie – P.E.I., Prince Edward Island.

Penobsquis – Kings County community that was named during the coming of the early railway line. Alan Rayburn mentions that the name may be related to the Maliseet Penobsq and suggests that it translates as "stone brook."

Petit Large – Wilderness campsite at Kouchibouguac National Park.

Pets de soeurs – Acadian cinnamon rolls that are also nicknamed nun's buns, nun's farts, and old women's bellybuttons.

Petty – Village of Petitcodiac that was once known as Head of Petitcodiac.

Pettyrochay – Petit-Rocher in Gloucester County.

Philadelphia lawyer – Someone who makes things convoluted and unnecessarily complex.

Picaroons – Craft beer-maker in Fredericton who makes an excellent bitter and Irish Red.

Picture Province – Old license plate motto.

Piece of tail – Sexual intercourse.

Pieces – Logs, as in ninety pieces a load.

Pigs in blankets – Broiled oysters wrapped in bacon.

Pirate Lake – York County lake near the Chiputneticook Lakes on the Maine border.

Pissed off – Upset.

Pitch dark – Really dark.

Plaster Rock – Victoria County community on the Tobique River that was named for the local red gypsum.

Platform man – In early-twentith-century politics, a good platform man was a great political talker on the election circuit.

Les Ployes – Buckweat pancakes that are featured at the La Foire Brayonne Festival at Edmundston. The record is seventeen pancakes eaten by one person in seven minutes.

Plumpers – Nickname for Spanish gold coins that were reportedly awash on the beaches for many years near Point Lepreau after the British brig HMS *Plumper* went down during a northeaster gale in 1812. The vessel was known to have on board at least £70,000 of gold and silver coins.

Plumsweep – Kings County community near Sussex originally called Salmon River but was changed to avoid duplication with many other sites of the same name.

Poachers – Hunting and fishing out of season, or fishing with a net, hunting at night with a light, etc. (See also Jacking)

Pocologan – Community and harbour in Charlotte County that was named from the Passamaquoddy term Pekalugan, meaning "enclosed harbour."

Poet's Corner of Canada – Fredericton. Named in honour of three famous Canadian poets: Bliss Carman, Sir Charles G.D. Roberts, and Francis Joseph Sherman. Born in or near Fredericton, these three poets were educated at the Univeristy of New Brunswick and are buried in the Forest Hill cemetery.

The Point – Many places have been simply known as "the point" in New Brunswick, including Rocky Point and Reeds Point, but one of the oldest in the province is Pointe-du-Chêne on Shediac Bay, once known as Oak Point.

Point de Bute – Site near the Nova Scotia border. From the French Pointe à Buot.

Pokiok – York County community and stream on the St. John River. Named after the Maliseet Pokweok, which means "a narrow place or gorge."

Politics in New Brunswick is a deadly game – Observation by R.A. Tweedie, a supreme political behind-the-scenes operator from 1935-1960. (See also Hell hath no fury like a politician scorned)

Pollett River – Westmorland County river that flows into the Petitcodiac and was named after Peter Paulet, a Mi'kmaq elder who was widely known throughout southeastern New Brunswick in the mid-1800s.

Pony – Anything smaller than normal.

Poontang – Sexual intercourse.

Poor as church mice – Mouse poor is very poor and church mice are even poorer.

Porcupines – Baked coconut, sugar, and butter balls.

Portage – Route over high ground between two streams where canoe and cargo are carried.

Portashers – From the word "portage" but the reference is to men who delivered the camp supplies from the company store to the lumber camps.

Potato belt – The upper St. John River valley where the majority of New Brunswick's commercial potato industry is located. This section of the valley is also called the Bible Belt.

Potato bug – Dreaded insects that infected the crops in

some way almost every season. Picking the bugs off the leaves would sometimes work for a day or two but old-timers claimed a substance called Paris Green would rid the crops of the pest.

Potatoes in their jackets – Potatoes served with their skins on.

Pot-en-pot – An Acadian fricot, a stew-like dish that contains meat and potatoes and is cooked on top of the stove.

Poutine râpée – An Acadian dish of grated potato wrapped into a ball around a minced pork core.

Prayer Mountain Retreat & Motel – Lutz Mountain Inn near Moncton.

Pré-d'en-Haut – Westmorland Acadian community near Memramcook that has been translated as "meadow on the ridge."

Pretnear – Pretty close.

Preventatives – Government men hired to crack down on bootleggers in the early days of Prohibition. They eventually gave up and called in the Mounties.

Pudding in a Bag – Popular Acadian dessert (Poutine en Sac) that is sometimes called steamed pudding and is served with fresh cream.

Pugmoushers – One who is from Pokemouche on the North Shore.

Pull and be damned narrows – Site on the Letang River near St. George in Charlotte County where frustrated canoe paddlers have had difficulty going forward.

Pull the middle – In a logjam, drivers would often attempt to "pull the middle" in order to loosen the key logs so the flow could continue downriver.

Pulp peeler – Hard job, worse than driving a pulp wagon or truck, plus you usually received the nickname "peelhead."

Pump House – Craft beer brewery and restaurant on Orange Lane in Moncton. Makers of the popular Cadian Cream Ale.

Puncheon – Barrel of molasses.

Purple violet – The floral emblem of the province.

Push-an'-be-damned – Treacherous stretch of rapids on the upper part of the Southwest Miramichi River above Slate Island.

Put in the monkey wrench – Screwing it up.

Put the boots to her – Extra efforts to get it done.

Put the kettle on – Make tea or coffee.

Putting on a feed-bag – Sit down for a big supper.

Putting on airs – Acting pretentious.

Putting on a spread – An elaborate meal.

Putting on the dog – Elaborate affair but also pretentious.

Putting the kibosh on it – Stopping it.

Put your damper down – Clamp down or tighten up.

Q

Quaco Bay – Along the Bay of Fundy in Saint John County. The name is derived from the Mi'kmaq Goolwagek and means "haunt of the hooded seal," according to William Hamilton, author of *Place Names of Atlantic Canada*.

Quahog – Giant edible clam (grosses coques) found along the Northumberland Strait.

Quebec heater – Round, cast-iron stove made by the Enterprise Foundry in Sackville.

Quill her – Old midwife trick to encourage a late birth witnessed by the late Dr. Everett Chalmers. Find a tail feather from a hen, shear it till there is only a tuft left, and place the tuft up the nostril of the pregnant woman's nose. An explosive sneeze delivers the baby. Chalmers was a noted physician and surgeon in Fredericton, where the hospital is now named after him.

Quispamsis – Kings County community. The name is probably Maliseet in origin and can be translated as "little lake."

R

Racket – Unwanted noise but also can be a scam.

Rage for dipping – Sarcastic description of nineteenth-century water baptism by the New Lights, an early Baptist sect.

Ragged cabin – Log cabin with ends not trimmed.

Ragging on it – Will not give up and keeps bringing it up when no one wants to hear about it.

Rain before seven, fine before eleven – Weather prediction.

Raising a boil – Raising a salmon to the surface of the water in search of a fly, a fly-fisherman's dream because a boil appears seconds before the fish strikes.

The Range – Depression-era site along the Richibucto Road between Fredericton and Minto that was home to a huge make-work camp. At one point in 1933, 1,500 out-of-work men lived there in tents, cutting trees and building roads.

Rappie Pie – Well-known Acadian meat or fish, and potato dish (Râpure) that is baked in the oven and is actually more popular with Acadians in other parts of the Maritimes.

Rared – Reared

Rat's nest – A heap of trouble, as in "This is turning into a real rat's nest."

Ready Brewery – West Saint John's famous old brewery, the forerunner to Moosehead. (See also Moosehead Beer Company)

Red Rose Tea is Good Tea – Well-known advertising slogan for Red Rose Tea of Saint John.

Red sky at night, sailors delight but red sky in the morning, sailors take warning – Old mariner's prediction.

Reggie's – Old Germain Street diner in Saint John. Home of the Bagel Burger.

Renous – Community and river in Northumberland County. The name is derived from the Mi'kmaq chief Renou or Renard.

Republic of Madawaska – Mythic republic that became a popular notion throughout Madawaska County when three regions – Quebec, Maine, and New Brunswick – all claimed Madawaska. Unwilling to choose, citizens proclaimed a republic and themselves Brayons, derived from their French ancestors who grew linen (brayage) flax.

Restigouche Sam – Campbellton's icon, the giant twenty-eight-foot steel salmon statue.

Restigouche Toothpick – Campbellton's first newspaper, founded in 1886.

Resurgo – Moncton's motto, "I rise again." The town was incorporated in the 1850s, but suffered financial setbacks prior to Confederation (1867) and was forced to deincorporate and abandon town status. After attracting the Intercolonial Railway in the 1870s, Moncton came back and became a city in the 1890s.

Resurgo over again – After losing thousands of jobs in the late 1970s due to the closure of Eaton's and the CN Railway Shops, Moncton came back again, and is now the fastest growing city "east of Montreal."

Revenooer – Customs officials or revenue agents.

Reversing Falls – Saint John site that was named by Sir Charles G.D. Roberts. One lady visiting Saint John and under the impression that the falls on the St. John River were indeed reversible walked up to the gatehouse attendant and inquired, "Are you the man who reverses the falls?" Twice a day, tidal changes near the mouth of the river reverse the river flow so the current changes in the opposite direction.

Richibucto goose – This goose is a fish: salt shad.

Rich like Sam Napier – In 1857, Samuel Napier of Bathurst discovered a 145-pound gold nugget in the Australia gold fields and managed to get the nugget to England, where it was put on display at the London Crystal Palace exhibition. Napier returned to the North Shore a prince but died a pauper in 1902.

Ride the rods – Old hobo practice of riding the truss rods of trains.

Right out of 'er – Could be used as an expression for drunkenness, as in "We got right out of 'er," or describing someone who appears deranged or out of control.

Right through your bones – Damp and cold Maritime weather.

Rink rat – Hanger-on around the local rink. Also, wharf rat.

Riparian rights – Unique New Brunswick right that involves fishing privileges for a person who owns certain property bordering a body of water. Water rights for riparian owners became enshrined in Canadian law after a 1912 legal case established that riparian rights on the Nepisiguit River had been infringed upon by pollution created by a mining company. Throughout the twentieth century, New Brunswick became the battleground for the full extension of riparian rights with New Brunswicker Gérald V. LaForest writing the defining text that outlined common-law rights of riparian owners in eastern Canada. LaForest was a judge of the Supreme Court of Canada from 1985-1997.

Ripples – Sunbury County community close to Minto that is named after the rapids in the nearby Little River.

Rips – Term for rapids, especially in southwestern parts of the province such as Meetinghouse Rips.

River Glade – Community in Westmorland County. Also nearby is The Glades. When the early settlers appeared in southeastern New Brunswick, this area was described as low-lying and covered with grass.

Rivière-du-Portage – Site in Northumberland County where it was necessary to portage canoes while travelling along the Miramichi River system.

Robbing Peter to pay Pierre – Anti-French slogan from the 1960s developed during the Charlie Van Horne Conservative campaign to try and stop Liberal Louis Robichaud and his Equal Opportunity program that was designed to bring additional services to the northern part of the province comprised of a majority of Francophones. (See also Equal Opportunity and Little Louis)

The Rocks – Hopewell Rocks, an Albert County site on the lower Petitcodiac River where flowerpot rocks have been shaped by huge Bay of Fundy tides. They're called flowerpots because of the trees, grass, and flowers growing on the huge sandstone rocks that seem to float in the water at high tide.

Rockwood Park – Saint John city park. Writer David Goss has looked into the history of how Rockwood Park got its name and he writes, "Rockwood Park is a trail- and lake-studded 2,600-acre mix of woodland to the north of Saint John, and is in fact a part of the city. It is often said to be the largest such city park in Canada; though this is not true today, it once was and the reputation has stuck. When the Horticultural Association first began putting parcels of land together to form the park in 1894, they had little money to work with, and conceived the idea that the park could be named by public vote, with each vote costing citizens twenty-five cents. Four names were available to the voters, namely, Victoria, (after the Monarch of the day, of course) Lily, (due to the great growth of lilies on the twenty-three-acre lake named after them, Lily Lake,) Mount Pleasant, (Saint John's first suburb, and is adjacent to the park on the south side, and where one of its major benefactors, G.R. Pugsley, lived) and finally, Rockwood, which was so descriptive of the area's features, and also happened to be the name of the Pugsley estate on the south border of the new park."

Rolling dam – A dam without a sluiceway so that excessive water poured or rolled over the top. The community of Rollingdam is located in Charlotte County near Waweig.

Rough around the edges – A person who is less than smooth, not refined.

Rough-tongued – Bad mouth with lots of swearing.

Roushebucta – Richibucto. The Kent County settlement and river was named from the Mi'kmaq Lichibouktouck, meaning "the river that enters into the woods." In French maps dating from the seventeenth century, it appears as Regibouctou.

Roustabout – Unskilled labourer and all-round gofer.

Rubbage – Rubbish.

Rubby – Rubbing alcohol, lethal substitute for liquor that became popular in the 1920s, also called "rub-a-dub."

Rum row – Each city and town in New Brunswick had a seedy part of town and in the old days, these areas would be called rum row. But during the mid-1920s, rum row referred to a section of the Bay of Fundy between Yarmouth and Saint John where big rum carriers would anchor and off-load liquor into small fishing vessels that would sneak the contraband into New Brunswick and over the line into the U.S.

Running the roads – Out all the time partying, never home.

Run out the rum – Temperance Alliance slogan to encourage the enforcement of the liquor act during Prohibition. The slogan also included the following: "You drove it from the saloon now drive it from the cellar."

Runround – Secondary river channel where the passage is narrow or almost fades out.

Run the river – Canoeing phrase for paddling the river or running the rapids.

Rustigoushers – People from the Restigouche.

S

Sacking – To bring up the rear at the end of a log drive and to fetch the lost and tangled logs. Logs often got jammed up or the water was too low to float all logs. Consequently, men and horses were dispatched to do the sacking and dislodge the remaining logs on a stream. A sacking crew was known as the "rear crew" in Nova Scotia.

Saint Johner – Citizen of Saint John.

Salisbury Big Stop – The biggest and no doubt most hectic truck stop, restaurant, and all-round pit stop in New Brunswick and perhaps all of North America.

Salty Towers Tourist Home – In St. Andrews. Advertised as "something a bit different, unique alternative to traditional accommodations."

Samp Hill – Kings County site near Havelock. Samp is an Aboriginal name for coarse ground corn made into porridge and sweetened with maple sugar.

Saplin pine – Commercially useless small logs from pre-mature pine trees.

Saucy – Sassy.

Say hi for me – Pass on my regards.

Scaler – One who measures cut logs or sawn lumber. A very important position in the lumber industry since the count determined the pay and that could be controversial if the scaler was dishonest or a bit greedy. (See also Thirty for a thousand)

Scantling line – Working with small timber pieces too tiny for boards or deals.

Scarce as hen's teeth – Very rare.

Scoudouc – Community and river near Moncton. Mi'kmaq in origin (Omskoodook) and refers to the river but meaning is unclear.

Scow – Large flat-bottomed boat used to transport freight down a river.

Second cousin twice removed – Not sure but related somehow.

Seenar – CNR, Canadian National Railway.

Selling down the river – Selling something out or screwing over by making a fast buck, as in "They're selling New Brunswick down the river."

Selling wet in a dry – Prohibition phrase for bootlegging alcohol out of a retail dry goods store.

Semiwagon Meadows – Stream and meadows in Northumberland County near the Southwest Miramichi River.

Serpentine – Northumberland County river and lake with features that resemble a serpent.

Set the dogs – Dogs were pointed iron grips that held a log in place on the sawmill carriage while the log was cut. A dogger would be in charge of "setting the dogs."

Setting-pole – A long pole that was used by river guides to transport canoes up and down the big salmon rivers of northern New Brunswick. The best poles would be iron-shod at the end for better traction, and a debate raged as to whether the salmon were disturbed by the thud of the iron hitting the rocky river bottom. Eventually, the outboard motor replaced the traditional setting-pole.

Sevogle – Community and river in Northumberland County. Name is Mi'kmaq and means "with many cliffs."

Sex-in-a-pan – Stuart Trueman's expression for his favour-ite dessert: layered pie. Trueman (1911-1995) was a well-known humourist, journalist, and historian.

Shack whacky – Cabin fever, shut indoors.

Shad – Boney fish not really worth the trouble of picking out the bones, as opposed to gaspereau that are also boney but worth the effort.

Shampers Bluff – Kings County community on Belleisle Bay. Named after a Loyalist family called Schomber or Shampier.

Shantyboys – This expression has its origins overseas or in the American Midwest. A shanty was a common name for a small hovel or poor house and in New Brunswick usually meant a lumber camp but could also be a camp for railway construction workers.

Sheldrake Island – Island at the mouth of the Miramichi River that was named after a local species of duck.

Shemogue – Community on the Northumberland Strait. Derived from the Mi'kmaq term Simooaquik, it can be translated as "a good place for geese."

Shenanigans – Tricks, practical jokes, as in "Let's have none of your shenanigans."

Shepody Bay – Body of water located at the mouth of the Petitcodiac River. The name is derived from the Mi'kmaq Esedabit. During the French period, the area was known as Chipoudy.

She's right off her rocker – Off base, as in not riding her rocking chair right.

Shilly-shallyed – Being less than forthright and evading responsibility.

Shim – A wedge to right an uneven surface, as in "Let's shim it." A shimshack was a shim storage shed on a railway line.

Shippagan turkey – Salt cod.

Shiretown – Capital of a county in the old local system of government. New Brunswick is divided into fifteen counties and thus had fifteen shiretowns.

Shit hit the fan – Spreading it around, as in everyone was affected.

Shittyack – Shediac. Sixteen variations are to be found on early maps including Chediac, Shediak, Jediack, Enpedediac, Chedaique, and Judayque. From the Mi'kmaq Esed-ei-ik and meaning "running far in."

Shoofly – Temporary railway track erected around an obstacle.

Shooks – Wood pieces that are either tops, sides, or ends and produced in sets to be assembled into boxes or barrels.

Shooting the breeze – Talking about this and that, nothing important.

Shore – Any coastline on salt water.

Short line – Railway term for any branch line connecting a town or construction site to the main trunk line. Shorts are railcars that are used exclusively on branch lines.

Shunting – Marshalling or switching railway stock in a certain order by moving the stock back and forth between a mainline and a siding, or bumping back and forth in a shunting yard. Shuntmen would work the yards.

Shy-la – Sheila, Gloucester County. Named after a woman whose family built a sawmill there prior to 1900.

Sit-down supper – A somewhat formal dinner where all diners are served sitting down.

Skedaddle – To run away. Skedaddle Ridge, Carleton County, was named to commemorate a group of Americans who had settled there after fleeing the Union military draft during the American Civil War.

Skidding – Piling logs in lumberyards by inserting skids between the rows, creating a skid-pile (logs in tiers squarely across the pile).

Skoodowabskook – Maliseet name for Longs Creek above Fredericton while nearby Kelly's Creek was Skoodo-wabskooksis. In James DeMille's (1837-1880) classic poem, "Sweet Maiden of Passamaquoddy," are the famous lines "in New Brunswick we'll find it / A sweetly sequestered nook / Where the swift-gliding Skoodowabskooksis unites with the Skoodowabskook."

Sleepers – Railway ties used to support the rails.

Slip and go easy – Old-fashioned buckwheat pancakes from the Southwest Miramichi region that often had the frustrating habit of sliding right off the plate.

Sloven – Low-slung wagon that was developed in Saint John to allow for off-loading cargo from scows that were resting on the tidal mud flats at low tide.

Slower than cold molasses – Very slow, but not as slow as cold molasses going uphill in freezing weather!

Sluice – An open-top water trough made of wood and designed to transport water over distance.

Small potatoes – Minor problem, no issue.

Smart as a whip – Very smart.

Smashers – Pre-Confederation political reform group led by Albert James Smith, "the Bull of Westmorland," and opposed to the established Family Compact system of government, what he called the "oligarchy of privilege."

Smoker – Northumberland County brook that feeds into the Northwest Miramichi River.

Snickers doodles – Tasty treats made out of graham wafers, dates and nuts, and according to the well-known humorist Stuart Trueman were often served at rural get-togethers such as sewing circles.

Sniffing around – Checking it out.

Snob hill – Where the rich live.

Snow and rain – What everyone talks about but no one does much about.

Snoozer – Railway sleeping car where you could reserve a roomette for overnight sleeping.

Some good – Very good.

Some piece of work – Derogatory description of a person.

Song of the Reel – George Frederick Clarke's best-loved book chronicling the supreme joys of fly-fishing the majestic rivers of New Brunswick. Clarke (1883-1974) was a Woodstock dentist, author, historian, archaeologist, sport fisherman, and conservationist.

Sonofa'hore – Swearing, as in son of a . . . whatever.

South Dead River – Near the Tobique River in Victoria County.

Sparking – Courting in nineteenth-century New Brunswick. Frances Beavan writes in her 1845 book *Life in the Backwoods of New Brunswick* that a young man would, "arrayed in his best go-to-meeting style, gear up his sleigh, and what with bear skins and bells, fancying himself and appearances enough to charm the heart of any maid or matron in the back woods, set off to spark Grace Marley."

Speak of the devil – Greetings to a friend who just arrived.

Speed the plow – Agricultural motto from York County associated with community fairs and bountiful harvest.

Spem Reduxit – Provincial motto that translates as "She restored hope" or "Hope was restored." The reference is to Britain, who agreed to the establishment of a separate New Brunswick colony in 1784 after the United Empire Loyalists, refugees from the American Revolution, had arrived.

Spiked boots – Lumber boots with steel spikes that allowed loggers to dig in and hold onto floating logs while working with their peavies to untangle a log boom.

Splitterman – Sawmill employee who separates the sawn boards after the log has passed through the saw. This work can be dangerous.

Sport – A come-from-away fisherman or hunter who must hire a New Brunswick guide in order to fish or hunt.

Sprills – Nickname for evergreen needles on the Miramichi, as mentioned by Herb Curtis in his novel *The Americans Are Coming*.

Spring burn – During the first dry spell each spring, settlers would light fires to burn the chopping that had been cut the previous year. Once burned, the blackened chopping became a scene of desolation that needed to be cleared of brush and burned off again. Now plowing and planting could begin.

Spruce beer – A low-alcoholic brewed concoction made from spruce bark, molasses, water, and yeast and used to fight scurvy in colonial times.

Spruce gum – Nature's chewing gum obtained by picking wads off the black spruce tree. In the late-1800s a company in St. Stephen sold the stuff commercially, claiming it to be the "world's best, pure gum."

Spruce partridge – No-good-for-eating bird that hangs out in fir trees as opposed to the tasty birch partridge that hunters prize.

Spuds – Potatoes.

Spy Lady from Magaguadavic – Sarah Emma Edmonds,

alias Franklin Thompson, an American Civil War soldier and a secret Pinkerton agent. Edmonds (1841-1898) was born in Magaguadavic. Disguised as a man, she joined the Union Army as Franklin Thompson in Michigan in 1861, serving as a spy, field nurse, and soldier. She wrote a book of her adventures – *Nurse and Spy in the Union Army*.

Squeal – To tell on someone, as in "You squealed on her." Also, to squeal your tires, meaning to "lay on the rubber."

St. Stephen – The religious connotation for naming this Bay of Fundy community is a bit far-fetched. According to J. Clarence Webster, a popular member of an early surveying crew was named Stephen and "Saint" was added as a "facetious gesture."

Stave – A thin piece of wood that is placed edge to edge with other staves to produce a barrel or cask.

Stick in the mud – Not having fun. Someone who refuses to allow themselves to have fun or join in.

Stiff-necks – Uptight.

Stogging – To stog is to fill moss between logs in a log cabin in order to insulate and tighten up the building. Stogging is also a term used to describe eating a hearty meal.

Stoker – Fireman on a steam locomotive.

Storm-stayed – Postponement overnight because of weather. To be obliged to remain where you are because travel is dangerous or impossible due to a storm.

Straggle bug – Nickname for a suspension footbridge that would be strung over the Northwest Miramichi River each spring.

Struck out – Headed off with a purpose, as in "We struck out for the coast."

Stuck up – Thinking you are better than everyone else.

Stuffed shirt – One who is prim and proper.

Stumping – According to wordsmith Bill Casselman, the dean of odd Canadian words, in old-time New Brunswick, stumping was a backwoods' method of announcing one's engagement. A note would be place in the nook of a stump along a cord road where neighbours passing by would stop and read the announcement.

Subway – Controversial (at the time) and now a Moncton icon on Main Street allowing CN trains to pass through the centre of the city.

Sugarbush – In her book *Life in the Backwoods of New Brunswick*, Frances Beavan writes, "The rock maple is the species particularly used for sugar, and perhaps a thousand of these trees near together constitute what is called a sugarbush."

Sugaring off – Boiling the watery maple syrup to produce pure maple syrup on a forty to one ratio.

Sugarline – Boundary of a maple sugar operation, i.e., where the sap line ended.

Sugarloaf Mountain – Few today can appreciate why a mountain would be named sugarloaf but years ago, sugar was sold in cone-shaped loaves that would be broken up before being used.

Sunday-go-to-meeting – Proper church day affair that required dressing up in formal wear.

Sunny bubbles – Teasing someone.

Superficial foot – Board measure of one foot of lumber, one square foot, one inch thick.

Sussex Ginger Ale – Once New Brunswick's favourite soft drink that originated, of course, in Sussex.

Swampers – Men who built temporary winter roads for hauling lumber by clearing brush, tamping down the earth, and sometimes pouring water over the road to create a hard frozen surface.

Swamp soggin – Hearty pudding made with molasses and flour, served in lumber camps.

T

Taffy pull – Molasses or maple candy that is heated and twisted into a rope-like candy.

Take a hike – Get out of here.

Take off, eh – Let me alone.

Taking tea – Afternoon tea-drinking get-together.

Taking the liquor cure – Swear off drinking, also known as "going on the wagon."

Taking the mud – Huge tides around the Bay of Fundy meant that the waterline could fluctuate over twenty feet at the docks and waterfronts. Only vessels capable of "taking the mud" (sinking into the mud and refloating undamaged) were able to take on freight at low tide.

Tall tale – Story that exaggerates the truth.

T&T – The Moncton *Times & Transcript* newspaper.

Tantramar – Great salt marsh near Sackville once known as Tintamarre, perhaps because of the racket from thousands of wild geese and other marsh fowl. Later, Tintamarre was anglicized to Tantramar.

Tanty-Wanty – Small stream near Geary in Sunbury County. Local settlers were from Niagara and the name has been derived from that of a small brook near Niagara called Tanawanda.

Tarry – To wait, as in "We could tarry no longer."

Tart – A flirt.

Tavrin – Tavern.

Taymite – Someone from Taymouth on the Naskwash River.

Teamster – Man who drove a team of horses.

Teddy Baseball – Nickname for Ted Williams, baseball great and supreme promoter of all-things New Brunswick, especially the Miramichi and its salmon fishing traditions. Williams fished on the Miramichi for years.

Tee it up – Set it up.

Teetotal Settlement – Old name for Cork in York County that was once an alcohol-free community.

Teetotalism – Temperance movement aimed at stopping all consumption of alcohol in New Brunswick. It began in the 1830s and ended as a movement (New Brunswick Temperance Alliance) in 1930.

Temperance Vale – Upper York County community that was named in honour of the nineteenth-century temperance movement.

Tempest in a teapot – Small matter that is being overplayed.

Tender – Assistant to the teamster, the main horse driver.

T'es pas serious – French-English slang for "You can't be serious."

Tétines de souris – "Breast of mousse," known in English as samphire greens and are among the best-known wild edible plants along the Fundy shore. The common name is glasswort, and the delicious little ferns usually appear in June after the highest spring tides have subsided.

TG – Saint John newspaper, *Telegraph Journal*.

That's a load of bull – A lot of bullshit from a bullshitter.

Them days – Prior years when things seemed better.

There's a knack to it – There's something special and a bit difficult to getting it done.

The Three Musketeers – Three Tory Members of the Legislative Assembly who publicly opposed Richard Hatfield's leadership of the provincial Conservative Party in 1985. Despite broad support, they failed to convince Hatfield to resign as leader and the party went down to total defeat in the 1987 election when Frank McKenna's Liberal Party took all fifty-eight seats in the legislature.

The Three Sisters – Trinity Lamps located in St. Patrick's Square on the lower end of Prince William Street in Saint John. The ornate iron lamps face the harbour to guide vessels into the city.

Thingomajig – Any odd tool or contraption and can also refer to sexual organs.

Thirty for a thousand – It took thirty trees to make a thousand board feet. About twenty New Brunswick trees would normally produce a thousand feet so thirty meant that something was wrong, the trees were small or the scaler (the man who measured the logs) was crooked. Legends about pre-Confederation New Brunswick claimed that the trees were then so large that "two logs made a thousand."

Three sheets to the wind – Out of control, as in drunk or plastered.

Three squares a day – Three meals a day and no worries.

Ticked-off – Not happy, disappointed and getting angry.

Ticker – Timepiece or watch. Also a nickname for the heart.

Tide wheel – Wheel turned by tidal action in a river.

Tidehead – Community on the Restigouche River where the tidal flow reaches its end.

Tie one on – To get loaded, as in drunk.

Time to feed your hay – Get ready for winter. Autumn switchover time when cattle are fed hay instead of the summer pasture grass.

Tin Fish Digs Tourist Home – Located in St. Andrews.

Tintamarre – Big racket festival. The final festival event at the annual Festival Acadien de Caraquet.

Tip of the iceberg – Beginning of something big (usually bad).

'Tis equal joy to come or stay – Lord Beaverbrook's favourite line from an old hymn that reflected his unwillingness to choose a favourite New Brunswick political party. (See also The Beaver)

Tit for tat – Equal trade-off.

TNB – Theatre New Brunswick.

Tobique – Victoria County river that flows into the St. John River, named in honour of Maliseet chief Noel Tobec.

Tom Kedgwick – Kedgwick River is a tributary of the Restigouche River. The name is Mi'kmaq in origin (Madaw-amkedjwik) but appears in some nineteenth-century maps as We-Tom-Kedgwick. The name was shortened to Tom Kedgwick and then to simply Kedgwick.

Tongue and groove – Lumber with shapes cut on alternate edges to produce a tight fit when fitted edge to edge, such as in flooring wood.

Too big for his britches – Attempting to show off or boast about one's abilities.

Took the cake – The epitome of something negative, such as the biggest problem or the worst crime, as in "That just took the cake."

Took the pledge – To sign a temperance society card promising not to drink again.

Torching herring – A traditional night fishing method around Passamaquoddy Bay that involved attracting the fish to the surface by means of flares held out over the dory and then scooping the herring into the boat. Aboriginal fishermen had developed this method of fishing long before Europeans arrived in North America.

Torst – Tourist.

Tote-road – A small hard-packed road through the woods where supplies would be hauled to a lumber camp. The toter was the hauler who drove the tote team.

Tough it out – Getting by with less than adequate resources.

Tough ticket – Hard-acting, hard-driving person.

Towline – Rope by which the horses towed the old timber rafts up to the landing grounds.

Trap smasher – A winter easterly gale that destroys fishermen's traps around Grand Manan and Passamaquoddy Bay.

Treenail – Large wooden nail for securing planks and beams, and called a "trunnel" by shipwrights.

Trimmer – A car-chasing train in a shunting yard assigned to recover cars that have gone astray. The engineer driving the trimmer is a car chaser.

Tronno – Toronto.

Trying to ride two horses at the same time – Unwilling to commit, trying to be all things to all people.

Turkey – Lumbermen's backpack that would carry their personal belongings.

Turn – A turn was one trip out and back from the woods to the lumberyard. The last turn of the day would be the last load delivered to the yard.

Twerp – A cocky jerk.

Twitching horse – Describes the best working horse for pulling fallen logs out of the brush and into the yards, an intelligent and good working animal.

U

UBS – United Book Stores. A chain of used book stores that started in Moncton.

UNB – University of New Brunswick, Fredericton. Established in 1785, UNB is the oldest English-speaking univeristy in Canada, and one of the oldest public universities in North America.

UNBSJ – University of New Brunswick, Saint John. UNB opened a branch in Saint John in 1964.

Underground Lake – High in the hills of Albert County, next to Demoiselle Creek, is a strange body of water about one hundred feet long. The lake can be entered through a cave and is surrounded by gypsum.

Uplifter – Old-time Baptist description for rock-solid member of the congregation, i.e., deacon or church elder.

Upper Canada – Ontario and Quebec. (See also Up yonder)

Upper Mistake – York County brook that flows into the Eel Lakes.

Upsalquitch – River and lake in Restigouche County that flows into the Restigouche River. Translated from the Mi'kmaq Apsetkwechk as "the little river" but may also have meant "narrow going" since the river is quite narrow in places.

Up the creek without a paddle – In a jam without an easy way out.

Up the hill – UNB. A reference to the fact that the University of New Brunswick in Fredericton is built on a hill overlooking the downtown portion of the city and the banks of the St. John River.

Up the stump – Pregnant, as in "He got her up the stump."

Uptown – Downtown Saint John or Saint John Centre as distinct from West Saint John, the south end, or other parts of the city.

Up yonder – Quebec, Ontario, Upper Canada.

V

Van Horne Bridge – Cross Point Bridge over the Restigouche River at Campbellton. Opened in 1961, the J.C.
Van Horne Bridge is also known as the Campbellton Inter-
provincial Bridge as it links the province with Pointe-à-
la-Croix, Quebec. It was built through the political efforts
of J.C. "Charlie" Van Horne, a larger-than-life figure in
New Brunswick politics who hit the 1960s campaign trail
wearing a white stetson and riding a horse.

Varmint – Small creature such as a rabbit.

Vegetable belt – Maugerville area along the St. John River
where the low-lying land is continually flooded by river
silt that leaves rich nutrients in the soil.

Velvet Siege – The capture of Fort Beauséjour in 1755.
French forces inside the fort were vastly outnumbered by
Colonel Monckton's impressive show of force, and thus
the fort fell quickly and without heavy fighting.

Very best – Wishing someone a good day, as in finishing a
conversation by saying, "The very best."

Volume – Valium, as in "Relax, take a volume."

W

Wake up bars – Highway bumps on the edge of the pavement that warn drivers they are headed off the road.

Walking boss – Not the main man but the little boss, who worked the timber yards with the rest of the workers. The walking boss often wanted to become the bull-of-the-woods and that usually meant having to dethrone the "Main Man." (See also Main John)

Wangan – "Down at the wangan." Storage box or chest for carrying personal goods to the lumber camps. Eventually, wangan became associated with storage shacks in lumber camps and along the waterfronts. Mike Parker in his book *Woodchips and Beans* notes that the term probably originated in Ontario lumber camps and was called the "wong'n box" in Nova Scotia.

Wares – Herring weirs around the Bay of Fundy. (See also Bushed)

Was a goner – I lost my way and thought I was a "goner."

Washademoak – Community and lake in Queens County near Codys. The lake is fed by the Canaan River and empties into the St. John. The name has been traced to the Maliseet Wasetemoik but it is not clear what the name stands for.

Watch for moose – Highway sign warning motorists to keep on the alert for moose while driving on the highways. Yielding to moose is also proper etiquette when travelling in the woods.

Watch-toi la – French-English slang for "You're treading on thin ice."

Waterhaul – Fishermen's term for having to stop and get fresh water, but also pejorative in that it meant coming home with practically nothing but water.

Waterloo Row – Fredericton's finest address that stretches along the St. John River and The Green. (See also The Green)

Went full-blast – Going full out, fast and hard.

Went into a lodge – A cut tree that has not dropped because it has fallen, or lodged, into a tree branch still standing. Also described as a clothesline by some lumbermen.

Westconsin – Wisconsin. Big woods where many New Brunswick lumberjacks went to seek their fame and fortune.

Wet behind the ears – Young and inexperienced.

We the People – Slogan of the Confederation of Regions party in the 1980s and 1990s. (See also COR)

Wet stuff – Prohibition-era expression for liquor, as in "We had the first great slosh of the wet stuff." Great amounts were landed along the Bay of Fundy coast for transportation into Maine beginning in the summer of 1925 and ending with the repeal of Prohibition in the U.S. in 1937.

Wheeler-dealer – Big guy always trying to make deals and sometimes not quite on the level.

When rum was king – Description of the Prohibition Era when most everyone drank or sold rum.

When the hauling breaks up – When the winter lumber season is over, there'll be no more yarding logs and back-breaking work.

White poultice – Old name for late spring snowstorm that farmers believed actually helped young crops grow as long as the snow melted quickly.

Who let the cat out of the bag? – Who told the secret? Also, who spilled the beans?

Whole kit and caboodle – Everything including the kitchen sink.

Whole nine yards – Everything, as in all the resources that can be mustered or the whole ball of wax.

Whole shebang – The works.

Whoops – Cries of "whoops" were a popular way to end a folksong around a campfire or in a lumber camp. Whooping can be traced to the Miramichi region and its unique folksong tradition that originated in the lumber and fishing camps.

The wife – Sexist reference to a female partner. Also, the little woman and the Missus.

Wigwag – Swinging signal at a railway level crossing.

Wild goose chase – Hopeless search or expedition.

Will o' the wisp – An odd natural phenomenon described

as dancing lights or fireballs that appear in swampy areas of the province and are believed to be forerunners of danger or death. Feu follet in French and esk-wid-eh-wid in Maliseet.

Winging it – Doing it on a whim and a prayer (without much thought).

With a ten-foot pole – Can't do it even with the help of a ten-foot pole.

With all the trimmings – Fancy dinner with special details.

Woe unto you, ye Bocabecers – Traditional curse placed on two heads of families in Charlotte County because they refused to stop lumbering and come out of the woods to bury their dead father.

Wolf it – Gulp it down quickly.

The Wolves – Rock-fanged islands off Deer Island that, according to an Aboriginal legend, were once Glooscap's dogs. With the arrival of the Europeans, Glooscap turned the dogs into rocks in order to guard the Bay of Fundy.

Wooding-up station – Shed along the railway line full of wood for refueling the early wood-burning locomotives that would burn a cord every thirty-five miles.

Woodpecker Hall – Kings County community near Hampton.

Woolastook – Maliseet name for the St. John River and means "good river" or "the good river for everything." The European nickname is the Rhine of America.

Worded – To write out the words to a song on paper.

Workshop – On the Miramichi, the term for the bedroom, according to acclaimed novelist and lexicographer Herb Curtis.

World's fastest human – Saint John speed skater Charlie Gorman, world champion in 1927.

World's longest covered bridge – Hartland Bridge, built across the St. John River in 1901.

Worry-pas – French-English slang for relax, don't worry.

Wound up and fit to be tied – Very uptight.

Y

Yangin – Loud noise.

Yankee toast – Frying old bread in a butter and molasses mixture.

Yard – Place where logs would be piled before being dragged to the riverbank to wait the spring log drive. Yarding would be gathering and piling up logs, but is also a term used when deer and moose tramp down the deep snow in late winter to create "yards."

Yawho – Cowboy, redneck.

Year without summer – The black summer of 1816 was caused by a volcanic eruption of Mount Tambora in Indonesia that produced a massive cloud of ash, cinders, and sulphur estimated to be in excess of 150 million tons. It was also called the poverty year since no crops grew.

Ying-yang – Stocking up, as in "I've got lots, in fact I've got it up the ying-yang."

Yogi Bear's Jellystone Park at Kozy Acres – Campgrounds at Woodstock.

Yoko Lake – York County lake. The name may have been Maliseet in origin but appears in nineteenth-century maps as Yahoo Lake.

You could shoot a cannon through her – Empty spot, as in "I went to the dancehall the other night and couldn't believe it – you could shoot a cannon through her – where was everyone?"

Youdeyem – Université de Moncton.

Young lads – Young fellows on the Miramichi.

Your cup of tea – Personal preference.

You're always welcome at Billy's – Slogan at Billy's Seafood Company, City Market, Saint John.

Your neck of the woods – Your neighbourhood or your town.

Your yap – Don't give me any of your yap (bull).

About the Author

Dan Soucoup is the author of *Historic New Brunswick* and a number of other publications, including the bestseller *Maritime Firsts*. He has worked in publishing and bookselling in the Maritimes for more than twenty years and writes a column, "Looking Back," for the Moncton *Times & Transcript*.

Other books by Dan Soucoup:

Maritime Firsts

Historic New Brunswick

Maritime Book of Days

Glimpses of Old Moncton

Edwardian Halifax

Looking Back

McCully's New Brunswick